LAW, JUSTICE AND DEMOCRACY

LAW, JUSTICE AND DEMOCRACY

•

LORD McCLUSKEY
SENATOR OF HER MAJESTY'S COLLEGE
OF JUSTICE IN SCOTLAND

SWEET AND MAXWELL
BBC BOOKS

Published by BBC Books
A division of BBC Enterprises Ltd,
Woodlands, 80 Wood Lane,
London W12 0TT

and

Sweet and Maxwell Ltd,
11 New Fetter Lane,
London EC4P 4EE

First Published 1987

British Library Cataloguing in Publication Data

McCluskey, John Herbert, Baron
Law, justice and democracy: the Reith
lecturers 1986.
1. Judges—England
1. Title
344.207'14 KD7285

ISBN 0 421 37890 5 (hardback)
0 563 20549 0 (paperback)

Typeset by Phoenix Photoseting, Chatham in 10/11½pt Bembo
Printed in England by Mackays of Chatham Ltd

CONTENTS

PREFACE

In the BBC Reith Lectures, 1986, I discussed relevant aspects of the role and character of our judiciary in the hope of assisting listeners to make their own judgments about the tasks that judges can and should perform in a mature representative democracy. This book contains a slightly revised version of the lectures, the style of which was chosen with the listener principally in mind. I am also now able to refer, more fully than I could in the broadcasts, to the words or the works of others and to acknowledge my indebtedness to them, whether or not I agreed with the views quoted. In some instances I have added to the broadcast text.

My researches took me to the United States of America and to Canada. In Washington I was greatly assisted in understanding the role and dynamics of the Supreme Court by the then Chief Justice of the United States, Warren Burger, and by his colleagues, Justices William J. Brennan, Lewis J. Powell Jr. and Sandra Day O'Connor. In Harvard I was welcomed and enlightened by Archibald Cox, formerly Solicitor General of the United States, Special Watergate Prosecutor and the Samuel Williston Professor of Law at Harvard. In Ottawa I was entertained and informed by the Chief Justice Dickson of the Supreme Court of Canada and his colleagues, and by Ed Ratushny, Professor and Director of the Human Rights Centre at Ottawa Law School. Judge T. F. O'Higgins, now a member of the Court of Justice of the European Communities in Luxembourg, helped me to appreciate the relevance of the Irish Constitution to the work of judges in the Republic of Ireland. Justice Michael Kirby of the Federal Court of Australia gave me Antipodean encouragement by providing me with a recording of his 1983 Boyer Lectures on ABC in which he interpreted the judiciary to an Australian radio audience. Professor Ian R. Scott, Barber Professor of Law at The University of Birmingham provided me with many insights into the workings of the law in England.

Professor I. D. Willock, Professor of Jurisprudence at the University of Dundee, gave me invaluable assistance by guiding my reading, accompanying me on the North American study visit, and constructively criticising my drafts. Lord Mackay of Clashfern and Lord Morton of Shuna were also kind enough to read the drafts and to make valuable suggestions.

My radio producer, Anthony Moncrieff, supplied me not only with all the help I needed to come to terms with the broadcasting itself but with excellent guidance on the avoidance of difficult legal jargon which a largely lay audience would find indigestible. George Fischer, Head of Talks and Documentaries Radio at the BBC also read the drafts and courteously steered me away from broadcasting errors.

I should like to express my gratitude to the Lord Chancellor, Lord Hailsham of St. Marylebone, to Lord Scarman and to Professor Ian Kennedy, for their permission to reprint the text of the Radio 4 discussion (broadcast, Sunday Februry 8, 1987) of certain of the main themes I addressed in the Reith Lectures.

My particular thanks go to the Board of Governors of the BBC for the privilege and opportunity of joining the ranks of my distinguished predecessors who made the Reith Lectures unique.

Finally, of course, the views expressed in these Reith Lectures are entirely my responsibility as are the errors which must have survived.

CHAPTER ONE

THE CHILL AND DISTANT HEIGHTS

•

If I were to be asked what temptations any new judge is exposed to, I should have to admit that they include arrogance, self-esteem and impatience. That answer must alarm all who know that the principal qualities a judge must possess are humility, modesty and tolerance. But just think of the facts. He has been elevated to a position in which he wields a royal authority. The apparatus of state lies ready to enforce his orders. The visible symbols of his office, the way he dresses, the place in which he sits, the manner in which he is addressed, the respect which he is accorded, all are designed to buttress that authority, to intimidate those who might wish to challenge or evade it.

But it goes deeper than that. He has seen it all before. After a quarter of a century of forensic jousting, he has emerged, in the estimation of those shadowy powers who decide such things, as the combatant best fitted to preside over future contests, deemed to possess the wisdom, the experience, the discretion to decide the rights and wrongs of his fellow citizens, to personify the majesty of the law. As he sits on the bench, observing the exposure, by the forensic process, of the frailties of litigants, pleaders, witnesses and malefactors, the whole scene tends to reinforce a sense of being placed above and superior to the struggle. Of course he knows that he is not, in fact, a superior being, but he is expected to comport himself as if he were. And these accumulated experiences encourage him to suppose that if he were to be given a freer hand and a larger canvas he could dispense a greater measure of justice, provide a more ordered way of regulating social conflict.

Even if judges are sensible enough – as I hope they are – to resist the intoxicating notion that they may be wiser, more dispassionate and surer-footed than their fellow men, others in society may seek to press them into a more intrusive, a more active role. I believe that, in a representative democracy such as ours, that would be a mistake. So I shall examine the role and character of our judiciary in the hope of assisting you to make your own judgment.

Let me start by asking: 'What do judges do?' To that question most people could offer an instant answer. After all, judges get a generous degree of media exposure as they send the wicked to prison, award large sums in damages or put an unexpected spoke in the wheel of some powerful bureaucratic machine. Occasionally, a judge attracts a degree of public attention, or even notoriety; but usually criticism is restrained, and respect freely accorded. Unlike most others who pronounce in the public domain, judges appear to offer, and to deliver, clear and definitive answers. Justice according to law is a coin which, when tossed, does not come to rest on the rim. It comes down heads or tails; it is clear who has won and who has lost. The judge gives his reasons, pronounces the result and withdraws to 'the chill and distant heights,'[1] constitutionally indifferent to the consequences. The litigants, and others, must adjust to the court's prescription, and order their affairs in accordance with it.

But the legal philosopher, the social scientist, the political activist, even from time to time the disappointed litigant, question this picture. They dare to assert, in the words of Warren Burger, lately Chief Justice of the United States, that 'unreviewable power is the most likely to self-indulge itself and the least likely to engage in dispassionate self-analysis'; and to conclude, as he did, that 'in a country like ours, no public institution, or the people who operate it, can be above public debate'.[2]

But is ours a country like his? Do our judges wield an unreviewable power? And should the judges join in the debate[3] about the exercise of judicial power,[4] or should they stay above it, adopting the attitude that God presumably takes towards theology? Well, of course, the judges in England and Scotland do not see their role as being in every respect similar to that of American judges. They do not claim to exercise an unreviewable power. They engage for the most part in rendering as between one citizen and another what is due to each, at the expense of the other. True, they make occasional forays into that less private border country where the citizen comes into conflict with the state or some lesser public authority. But politics, social engineering, the constitution; these are realms which the British judge would claim to enter with reluctance, and to quit with relief, just as soon as he has done the minimum that duty requires.

But judges know perfectly well that much of what they do – though not unreviewable – is likely to be final. For most cases are won and lost on the judge's view of the facts, not on subtle points of law.[5] Judges also know that if they do decide a substantial point of law in one case, that decision can determine the results in many others. And even if large numbers of the public don't care for the new twist in the law, there may be countless reasons why Parliament will not legislate on the matter. So some judges, on and off the bench, join in the debate. If they do, they may not readily persuade the other protagonists that their pronouncements are disinterested., They must hope to advance the argument not by reason of their authority but by the authority of their reasons.

The least that can be expected of one who might be branded an apologist is that he should admit his perspective. The judge should go further and acknowledge both his history and his limitations. The principal limitation, though it is also his strength, is the law itself. For under our system, the courts are bidden to do justice according to law. But at a purely functional level, each case demands a 'yes' or a 'no' answer. And when a judge begins to think that justice demands a 'yes' but the law requires a 'no', he has to stop and remember that judges have no general responsibility for considering the greatest good of the greatest number, or for advancing social or moral aims. Except insofar as such ideals are already woven into the law they apply, judges cannot think or judge in these terms. Justice itself is not a legal concept, but an extra-legal or pre-legal one. Insofar as he helps to build the just society, the judge's role is to be not an architect but a bricklayer.

It is for this role that, under our system, his training and experience are supposed to prepare him. Judges of High Court rank are appointed from the practising Bar. As advocates they will have spent perhaps 25 years before the courts, advising clients about the remedies they may seek or the claims they should resist. They will have advised how to avoid litigation or, if litigation proved inevitable, will have sought the acceptable compromise in order to escape the unpredictable risks, and costs, of a fight to the finish. When cases came to trial, they will have laboured to master the principles of other people's trades. As advocates, they will have marshalled the precedents that are helpful and found ways of differentiating the unhelpful, so that each client's case may be cast in a legally defined mould. If the first judgment went against them, they will have sought for flaws in the judge's reasoning, and if they believe they have found such flaws they will have attempted to persuade appeal courts of the errors of the lower court.

Occasionally, they will have engaged their forensic skills in litigations of high drama or deep significance. For, though most of their cases will have touched no one other than those directly involved, some, perhaps unexpectedly, will have produced results which for years to come affect the legal relations, the financial burdens or even the liberties of many who were unaware that the critical point was being litigated. So in one rather unlikely-looking case in 1929,[6] a Scotswoman, nauseated by finding a decomposed snail in a glass of ginger beer she was about to drink, was advised to pursue an action for compensation against the manufacturers and, by persuading the House of Lords that she had a good cause of action, changed the law for consumers throughout much of the English-speaking world.

And in 1980,[7] a Glasgow woman sought a court order to prevent the local water authority from adding fluoride to her domestic water supply; she argued on the facts that, as she no longer had teeth, fluoride could do her no good, but it might do her some harm; and on the law, she argued that Parliament had given no power to water authorities to put medicine in the water. She won the legal argument, but Parliament then changed the law[8] and enabled every water authority in the kingdom to add fluoride to its water supply; because the same court which gave her the legal victory also decided, as a matter of fact, that fluoride could do your teeth some good and your body no harm.

And recently an English mother, Mrs Gillick, raised an action to prevent health authorities from advising doctors that they could, without parental consent, prescribe contraception to girls under the age of 16.[9] She eventually lost her case, but obtained a judgment so phrased as to leave doctors and their patients perplexed as to the limits of the doctor's duty of confidentiality.[10]

From examples such as these, several things are clear. First of all, the courts may be called the 'courts of justice'; but the only justice they can offer consists of a limited portfolio of remedies such as damages, injunctions, declarators, divorce, custody, fines, imprisonment, and liberation; and the results, even of victory, can be wholly unexpected. And, secondly, in deciding each particular case, the courts are not trying to change society. They occasionally effect some sweeping change, but they cannot, at the time of decision, calculate realistically the social consequences of the rules they formulate.

If the lawyers guiding the litigants through the courts are partisan, as they must be, and spend their professional lives thinking in terms of precedents, rules and remedies, is it to be expected that the moment they don a judge's red robes they will suddenly acquire new habits of thought, new intellectual tools, new social perspectives? Of course it is not. Victory will indeed cease to be a goal because the judge espouses no one's cause. But the discipline of the law, the need to choose which litigant is entitled to what remedy, the intellectual habit of rationalising decisions, these are enduring imperatives that will influence all his decision-making.

And because the British judge is not an inquisitor, because he is not supplied with what the Americans call a 'Brandeis brief'[11] – a detailed study which seeks to set the law in its social and factual context and perhaps predict the social consequences of legal rulings – he must be slow to let his thinking be influenced by the real or apprehended consequences for others of what he decides for the litigants before him. And the British advocate, in devoting his professional life to advancing his clients' legitimate interests, regardless of his own preferences or prejudices, has kept his nose to the ground. So judges are not trained to leap in the air. When they do, it is usually to the detriment of the law. In short, the advocate is the father of the judge and neither is a social philosopher.

Courts do not choose what disputes come before them. Life and litigants choose the problems that judges are asked to resolve. It is largely a matter of chance whether or not the courts get the opportunity to answer any particular legal question, whether it is one that the legal profession was aware of or one that took almost everyone by surprise when it did come along and found an answer so totally unexpected that textbooks had to be rewritten. One such was *Rookes* v. *Barnard*, in 1963, when the judges of the House of Lords decided that an Act of Parliament – passed over half a century before – did not, in fact, confer upon trade unionists the immunities that most, till then, had thought it did.[12] So it took 57 years before the highest court in the country had the chance to explain that the Act did not mean what nearly everyone had understood it to mean.[13] So judges have to wait for cases; they cannot reach out and mould the law. Even if a judge has in his breast a sense of how the law ought to be, he cannot forage about for cases that will enable him to develop his doctrines.[14] He must sit and wait with such patience as he can muster. And the vast majority will go from appointment to retirement without more than a rare opportunity to write a bold new page in the lawbooks.

So, between them, the nature of practice and the haphazardness of opportunity put a blight upon reforming zeal. And knowing this, both as practitioners and as judges, they tend to concentrate on the intricate detail of the law, leaving the grand design to others. That is not a criticism. It is just a plain fact. Indeed, modesty is a wholly admirable trait in those who make a profession of directly ordering the lives and liberties of their fellow citizens. The legislator can think in terms of the greater good, but the judge's aspiration is to give the litigant his due.

There is yet another powerful constraint upon the judge one which conditions the way he thinks; it is his awareness of the precise, the unique facts of any case before him. In serious criminal cases, they are largely determined for him by a jury. In most civil cases he determines the facts for himself after the most meticulous examination of the available evidence. But in either event, his knowledge of the precise circumstances in which he comes to apply the law is likely to be profound.

It is this very feature of a judge's work that gives rise to the greatest public misunderstanding as to why a judge has imposed a particular sentence or decided a case in a certain way. Because, for the most part, and inevitably, the public are presented with only the sketchiest glimpse of the evidence. Indeed it is the common experience of those who take part in criminal trials that the press, in selecting what to report, prefer the bold evidence of guilt to the less dramatic sowing of doubt. How often have you been astonished, after reading reports of proceedings in a criminal trial, to learn that the accused has been acquitted? That is not because the jury have been bamboozled by techniques of persuasion. It is because the jurors, unlike the casual distant spectator, have heard the evidence, and observed the witnesses.

Similarly, because the judge in a civil case scrutinises the evidence with meticulous care and applies the law in a precise and detailed way which cannot be readily paraphrased, so the actual result will sometimes appear incomprehensible to those who see the result but don't trouble to study the reasoning.[15] And this essential feature of the judge's task, the application of existing rules of law to precisely established facts, makes a world of difference between the habits of thought of the judge and the habits of thought of the legislator. It is not just, as it has been put, that judges make law retail and legislators make it wholesale. The legislator prepares the pattern and hopes that the garment will fit all who come to wear it. The judge makes it to measure. The legislator tries to regulate the future. The judge mostly regulates the past.

Now I began by asking what judges do; and I shall not attempt a complete answer. But a fair summary might be this: a judge listens to other people giving evidence, which is extracted from them by lawyers who share with the judge a common understanding of the rules of evidence. Then the lawyers present arguments about what the evidence establishes, and bring to the attention of the judge such relevant rules of law as their own researches have discovered and invite the judge to give their clients the remedies they seek. The judge hears both sides. He passes all the material over his own well-calibrated mind, satisfies himself how the law applies to the established facts, and pronounces judgment which determines the rights and liabilities of the litigants. In short, he makes such decisions as are necessary in the light of the matters presented to him to declare which litigant wins and which loses. If several judges sit together, hearing cases on appeal, the facts are usually put before them in some pre-packaged form, and their real task is to consider if the law has been properly applied in the court below. So Appeal Court judges are routinely concerned with questions of law, sometimes abstruse, frequently intricate, occasionally entirely novel and seldom of great public interest or moment. But all the decisions of courts result from an interplay between particular facts precisely established in evidence, and law derived from Acts of Parliament or from the Common Law.

Now it might be thought that if that is all there is to it, there should really be no problems. Alas, that is not all there is to it. First of all, though in a perfect world it should not matter, some advocates are better than others, and many a sow's ear is made to look like a silk purse, to judge or jury alike. Secondly, the law does not have the quality of a railway timetable with predetermined answers to all the questions that human life, man's wickedness and the intricacies of commerce can throw up. One of history's greatest lawgivers, the Emperor Justinian, promulgated a Code of Law in the belief that it contained all the answers; he prohibited any commentary upon it in the hope that by preventing interpretation of its provisions the law would remain clear. It was a vain hope. The law, as laid down in a code, or in a statute or in a thousand eloquently reasoned opinions, is no more than capable of providing all the answers than a piano is capable of providing music. The piano needs the pianist, and any two pianists, even with the same score, may produce very different music.

Most cases that are fought to a finish are fought because, within the context of the rules, there is much to be said for both sides. Such cases are seldom hopeless till they're finished. One of Scotland's greatest judges, Lord Macmillan, believed that in most cases that were appealed it would be possible to decide the issue either way with reasonable legal justification.[16] Even on pure matters of law, today's heresy is tomorrow's orthodoxy.[17] That which is blindingly obvious[18] to one judge is seen by another as logically unsound. So, in the case about the snail in the ginger beer,[19] a principle of law which one Appeal Court judge characterised as 'little short of outrageous[20] was described by a Lord of Appeal as 'a proposition which I venture to say no one in Scotland or England who was not a lawyer would for one moment doubt',[21] only to hear two other Lords of Appeal disagree with him.[22]

In applying the law in any particular case, the judge is, to a surprising degree, free to make his own choice. It is not just that the law itself is often Delphic, or even that the facts can appear very different to different people. It is also because our system of justice allows judges a substantial element of discretion and choice which is only very lightly controlled. Although that discretion is exercised within the law, it is not wholly directed by the law.[23] And that at once raises the question: what are the influences that determine for any particular judge in any given situation the result of the extra-legal, the non-directed choice? It is difficult to escape the conclusion that the choices which the system leaves the judge free to make are influenced by the judge's personality, his instincts and preferences, his accumulated social and philosophical make-up and his sense of the public mood.

Consider a familiar example. The newspapers give saturation coverage to an outbreak of savage sexual assaults upon children. And while the storm is at its height a judge has to pronounce sentence in a case of child rape. The law gives him an enormous discretion. He can, in theory, order life imprisonment or 200 hours of community service. The system gives him that wide discretion because the judge who knows all the facts, including the background of the guilty man, is supposed to look at each case individually. He cannot look to the jury or the prosecution for guidance. The only plea the judge hears is one for leniency.[24] Then he is entirely alone. He knows that society is watching him. And he knows that he alone, at that moment, is charged by society with the power to mark, by the sentence he imposes, its sense of outrage, tempered by the justice of the case, by the wickedness and the frailties of the offender, and by the inability of the penal system to help either the offender or the victim in any meaningful way. He must disregard the fact that almost any sentence of imprisonment he imposes may be materially, but unpredictably, altered by administrative decisions which will take effect, years later, in circumstances he cannot foresee.[25] He can pronounce sentence in seven words or he can give an elaborate explanation of why he is doing what he does. He can deliver a sermon on the human condition. He can deploy his extensive vocabulary of words of censure, pity, revulsion, warning and threat. But, one way or another, from some inscrutable depths of his own gut, he has to make a choice which no rule of law compels. He is not just a machine. He is a person whose experiences, vanities, prejudices, certainties and doubts, however disciplined by training, cannot be wholly suppressed. In them he is unique. Through them he is different. If it were not so, judges would never disagree. One judge's self-evident truth would not be another's outrageous fallacy. The heresy of one generation would not become the orthodoxy of the next.

And, just as each judge is unique in his personality and outlook, so, collectively, judges broadly share experiences and perspectives that make the judiciary different. And this, I suggest, is a central and inescapable fact we must take notice of when, as a society, we decide how and even if we are to harness the talents of judges for social purposes that reach beyond the mere rendering to each litigant of what is his due. That fact is one I must assess when I come to consider whether we should enact an entrenched Bill of Fundamental Rights, and so confer upon our judges a new and enormous power. But, having raised it, let me return briefly to the judge's role in sentencing.

The judge is never answerable, whether to his fellow judges, to Parliament or to public opinion, for his decision. Of course he is not the Mikado, with despotic and arbitrary powers. His grosser excesses may be curbed on appeal.[26] But he cannot be called to account in the way an elected representative is. As an informed citizen, he is aware that the prisons are full.[27] He knows that it costs more to keep an offender in prison than to send a boy to Eton.[28] He knows that our prison regime does little to rehabilitate the miscreant,[29] and suspects that the sentences the courts impose have only a marginal deterrent effect.[30] He is conscious that nothing in his experience or background enables him to understand why most people commit most crimes, apart perhaps from obvious ones like theft.[31] He is not a penologist or a criminologist. He is uneasily aware of real disparities between sentences.

So when the judge sits alone, throwing his mental dice till they produce a figure that he subjectively feels will do, he knows perfectly well that the exercise is profoundly unscientific and owes more to chance than it properly should. He can hardly be reassured by the fact that what he is engaged in is commonly referred to as 'sentencing policy': the only real policy is to let the judges get on with it.[32] And the fact that he is answerable to no one within the limits of a large discretion, though it may make his task simpler, does not still his unease about the justice and effect of what he does. As Clausewitz said of strategy: 'It is simple, but it is not easy.' So it is with choosing between sentences of three years and seven years in jail.

Of course, someone has to decide, and if it has to be delegated to one man it is no doubt best to give the job to a person who knows the facts, who senses the going rate and who has no constitutional reason to look over his shoulder to gauge the likely reactions of those who have a policy, whether of retaliation or of clemency. But is that best good enough? I doubt it. Though non-lawyers are accorded a role in part of this field, through magistrates' courts, the lay public has no real role. In cases which have gone to trial, is there not an argument for seeking assistance from the very jury that has heard the whole evidence, and determined the fact of guilt? If the judge had the power to put before the jury the upper and lower limits of the range of sentences that he must consider, would not that enable there to be a lay participation in sentencing that would help to produce not only a more just result but a readier public acceptance of the result. We ignore at our peril public concern about disparity in sentencing between different courts and different judges.[33]

Courts hear ample evidence on guilt or innocence, but very little on the choice of punishment or disposal. Might not consideration be given to letting the public prosecutor suggest a sentence or a range of options, requiring him to produce reasons and perhaps evidence to support what he suggests, thus creating the beginnings of a true sentencing policy, the assumptions of which could be openly scrutinised and discussed in Parliament?

The public are told that sentencing is for the judges. That would be acceptable if judges uniquely knew what mystic principles guided their actions. But they don't. And it is the public who pay for prisons, who are the victims of crime, and who have to live in the community with and to maintain the families of offenders. Should the public have so muted a voice? It has frequently been suggested[34] that we should consider having a Minister of Justice, answerable to Parliament, whose responsibilities could include the development of a coherent, informed and even-handed sentencing policy, related to the resources, available and responsive to public concerns, to replace the present system under which largely untrained judges select from a limited clutch of unsuccessful expedients. It is not for a judge to assess, the arguments for such a step. I advocate no particular system. I merely highlight the primitive character of the one we have. But if the judges were relieved of responsibility for so-called sentencing policy, it could help them to play the role for which they are fitted, that of administering a system of law for which Parliament bears the responsibility.

The theme on which I end this lecture is the appropriateness of using judges to do what the present system requires them to do. The wisdom of setting them to entirely new tasks is another. To that I must return.

CHAPTER TWO

THE CLANKING OF MEDIEVAL CHAINS

•

In the first lecture I undertook to look at the role of our judges and at the character of our judiciary. I did so because we need to understand these matters in order to make a reliable judgment about whether or not we should confer upon judges a more active, a more interventionist role. Should we augment their power to make and unmake law? Should we empower them to review and even overrule laws made by Parliament?

So I asked what judges do; and reminded you that they decide the cases that happen to come before them. Of course they don't sit under a palm tree deciding each case as the fancy takes them or even as their subjective sense of justice suggests.[1] They decide according to law. Law and justice are not the same thing.[2] Justice is an abstract ideal whose precise content in any particular dispute is uncertain and debatable. By contrast, law is a kind of system, a collection of principles, makeshifts, fictions and expedients, none of them unchangeable, and most varying in character depending on the time and the place. So, at the simplest level, law is a tool designed to enable men to sculpt justice out of the raw material of life.

But it would be naive to rest content with that description. Law is a social instrument. It embodies and enforces moral, social, political, cultural and economic choices. It translates these choices into rules which are intended to realise both ultimate and intermediate social goals. It compromises these choices when they come into conflict. Often the choice is difficult and painful. A judge may find himself restricted to choosing which is the lesser of the two evils. So the links between justice and law are sometimes tenuous and indistinct. In a society like the United States of America, the law may be fashioned to uphold an individual liberal goal, such as freedom of speech – though it may achieve that goal unevenly[3] – and sometimes people have to pay a heavy price when others exercise that freedom.[4] In the Soviet Union, by contrast, the law closely censors individual expression, supposedly in the interests of some overriding public purpose. So again, at a price, the law is fashioned to achieve an end which is political in character. No doubt apologists for each system would claim that the object of the law was to realise some social purpose which, if pursued with sufficient vigour, opens the door to real justice. What would not be in dispute is that law is just a means to an end.

Individual judges in either country may not refer to justice by name, but, when applying the law to individual cases, the judges will claim, less pretentiously, to be acting in the public interest. It is hardly different in a society such as ours, where the boundary between free speech and restraint is jagged and indistinct: the law provides particular tools, such as obscenity, contempt, official secrets, blasphemy and defamation, and judicial notions of the public interest guide the hands that wield the tools. But just as 'the public interest' will not have the same meaning in different societies, it will not necessarily have the some content for different judges. In fact, a concept such as the public interest – like so many other broad concepts that open the door to judicial discretion – is imprecise and elastic, and compels the judge to make value-judgments which are not wholly dependent upon the letter of the law.[5]

So the next question is: how do judges think? Only a cynic would put the preliminary question: do judges think? But, as we brush aside the cynic's question, we should acknowledge that the application of the law to the facts in order to produce a decisive result does require thought. The contested and difficult case is almost always unique. The result is not preordained. The judge has to think what result the law indicates for these litigants in this case. And, when the law allows some room for choice, he has to think of principled reasons why he should make the choice he does.

So, how do judges think? Now if I were to ask, 'how do Americans think?' or 'how do engineers think?', you would instantly point out that there is no reason to suppose that all Americans think the same way. Or all engineers. Or even all or most American engineers. And, of course, it is equally true of judges. They think in different ways. Like the engineers, they must draw upon some common and agreed body of principles, though the principles available to judges, being man-made, are more flexible and can be altered.[6] Judges must disclose their thinking. They advance reasons to justify their decisions. And what is most striking about those cases – usually the most difficult, the most contentious, the most celebrated cases, in which several judges, or even several different levels of court in the appeal hierarchy, disclose their reasoning – is that the several judges give different reasons. Indeed, they frequently arrive at different results; and inevitably, when that happens, the reasons must be different.

In truth, and to state the matter comprehensively, they can arrive at the same result for the same reasons; they can arrive at the same result for different reasons; they can arrive at different results for different reasons; and – just occasionally – they can come to different results for what look like the same reasons. So, if we can assume that the judges are impartial, intelligent and logical and are searching for the legal answers within the same shared corpus of principles and precedents, with a view to applying the same law to the established facts, we are driven to the conclusion that the application of the law to the facts is not a self-contained logical process. Judges frequently say, when they give their reasons, that they have been driven or compelled or forced to come to a particular conclusion, sometimes without difficulty, sometimes with regret, sometimes with considerable doubt or hesitation; only to hear their colleagues announce that they have been driven, compelled, forced down a different road to a different conclusion. Thus, despite the common principles, despite a mountain of precedents, despite a tradition of trying to write into Acts of Parliament precise answers to all foreseeable situations, the judge is left remarkably free to follow his own route to his own conclusion. If I am right, in suggesting that the law and logic leave judges a freedom of choice which is real, both as to the result and as to the reasoning which is adduced to justify the result, does the reasoning contained in the written opinions of judges tell us the whole story? Or are there other assumptions, other considerations, other suppositions disclosed or undisclosed, visible or invisible, which judges individually or collectively hold to be self-evident and which are just as important as the close, analytical reasoning in which such opinions are so rich?

Let me look again at the celebrated case of Mrs Donoghue,[7] who drank some ginger-beer which a friend had poured into a tumbler from a dark-brown bottle. When the tumbler was being refilled, a dead snail floated out of the bottle. Mrs Donoghue was distressed. Seeking compensation for her upset, she pursued a case against the manufacturer who had sold the café proprietor the dark, sealed bottle containing both the beverage and the dead snail. Her claim raised a pure question of law: if the manufacturer of an article intends it to reach the consumer in the same state as he despatched it, without any opportunity for an intermediate inspection, does he owe to the consumer a duty to take care to ensure that the article is free from defect likely to cause injury? The law to be laid down for the manufacturer who bottled Mrs Donoghue's ginger-beer was going to be the law for every manufacturer whose product was intended to reach the consumer without intermediate inspection. And it could not logically be confined to manufacturers: the same principle should apply to those who negligently designed, constructed or even repaired buildings or machinery, or even to those, such as bankers or accountants, who expressed and communicated an expert opinion, and, by doing so, set in train a chain of events resulting in loss to persons to whom the opinion was communicated, even if these were persons with whom they had not contracted but who had placed reliance on the experts' care and skill.[8]

So Mrs Donoghue's case raised the spectre – or the bright new dawn – of product liability. In trying to derive a principled answer, the judges of the House of Lords analysed over 30 precedents, cases from different times and various countries. When the decision was announced, those precedents that fitted the result for which a judge would vote were quoted with approval. Those that did not fit were said to be different or were rejected contemptuously with words like those of Lord Buckmaster: 'Better that they should be buried so securely that their perturbed spirits shall no longer vex the law.'[9]

When it came to the principles of the law, the judges were equally divided. Some thought it would be 'little short of outrageous' to hold manufacturers liable to the victims of their negligence: Lord Tomlin reminded their lordships of a recent railway disaster – caused, apparently, by a defective axle – and expressed dismay at the possibility that the victims of the crash might be able to sue the manufacturers of the axle. Where would it all end? Others could see nothing but justice and common sense in a rule of law which made the careless manufacturer compensate those who were injured as a result of his carelessness. By a majority of only one vote, the judges of the House of Lords reversed the decision of the lower court, and chose to uphold the principle that the manufacturer was liable to the consumer for his negligence: and soon that principle came to be seen and almost universally accepted as the embodiment of obvious common sense.[10] But no one reading the written opinions of the judges and observing the rhetorical passion of the language used can be left with any doubt that the decision was not wholly dependent upon the reasoning, that the judges rationalised and pleaded like advocates for the view they had formed. The case is a striking example of how a mountain of precedents still leaves judges free not only to evolve or restrict a principle but even to create or destroy one. And of how judges, with precisely the same starting materials in terms of fact and legal tradition, end up crusading for diametrically opposite conclusions.[11]

It is not often that judges reveal the depth and character of their differences by resorting to such colourful and polemical language; but even when their disagreements are couched in the most urbane terms, the disagrements themselves are often highly significant. And not all disagreements reach the surface. If a court sees itself as an instrument of government or as the trustee or the promoter of some important public purpose, it may try to produce a united front, by delivering one opinion, called the Opinion of the Court. In the United States Supreme Court, unanimity had to be fought for by argument, negotiation, compromise and diplomacy before Chief Justice Earl Warren could announce the unanimous result in *Brown* v. *The Board of Education.*[12] This was the landmark case in 1954 in which the Supreme Court held that the segregation of white and black school-children in the public schools of a state violated the constitutional rights of black children. These rights had been created in 1868 by the 14th amendment to the American Constitution, after the North's victory in the Civil War. The Court refused to follow earlier decisions in which it had been ruled that racial segregation by public authorities was permitted by the Constitution. It was plain to the judges who took part in the case that to declare such segregation unconstitutional was to announce a revolution, to lay down a new law which millions of people and many states might resist, evade and even disobey; the force and authority of the new law would be gravely weakened if the Court did not speak with a single voice. So the unanimity of the Court became of the greatest importance, second in importance only to the making of the decision itself.[13]

That is an example of judges making unanimity itself a goal in order to avoid weakening the authority of the court's decision, an acceptance by judges of what, in political terms, would be called collective responsibility for what they realised was a decision of enormous political and social importance.

That, of course, is America. Our courts hardly exercise comparable governmental functions: the lack of unanimity among our judges matters less and seldom attracts attention. And disagreements do not always emerge: if the case is dull, if the court is one from which there is no appeal, or if the judge who disagrees does not feel sufficiently strongly to sit down and write out a detailed dissent. But, despite the various influences that might discourage a declaration of dissent, the differences that can emerge are remarkable. In the snail in the ginger-beer case, the judges were almost evenly split as to the result.[14] In Mrs Gillick's case[15] the nine judges who considered the case split 5:4 in favour of Mrs Gillick, but in the House of Lords the voting was 3:2 against her. She lost. In the case in which the Defence Secretary sought delivery from *The Guardian* of documents which Sarah Tisdall had copied and leaked to that newspaper, the House of Lords split 3:2 against *The Guardian*.[16] And in a case in 1971, no three of the five judges who had heard the case in the House of Lords could agree. So Lord Diplock, in order, as he said, to avoid discredit on the administration of justice in the United Kingdom, voted with two other judges in order to provide a majority, even though he disagreed with their opinion.[17]

So, judges do think. They study the results of earlier cases and the reasons given by the judges for reaching those results; they seek to discover and to articulate the principles which those earlier judges must be deemed to have had in their minds when they reasoned their ways to the results in those cases. But judges are not engaging in some inexorable exercise in which every choice is determined by existing law. Choice there is, but often not the choice between the right answer and the wrong answer.[18] Between them, law, reason and discretion leaves judges free to declare results which derive at least in part from philosophies, attitudes and influences which are not themselves rules of law. It is unnecessary for me to assess the argument advanced by others that the judiciary is biased in its choices and prejudiced in its decisions because of the narrow social, educational and professional background which most judges share.[19] It is enough to acknowledge that no one can be entirely free of the perspectives and assumptions that derive from his background. No matter what the law puts into a novel case, a judge can always take a little more out. So, although judges do not normally profess to legislate, it is inescapable that courts make law.[20] The common law was made by judges. Every time a court determines the result in a particular case by redefining and developing legal principles and rules in which a way as to ensure that they will govern future cases, it is performing a function which resembles the legislative function. Let me illustrate this.

Parliament legislated that when damages for personal injury were being calculated, certain sums received by way of invalidity pension were to be deducted from the plaintiff's damages.[21] By contrast, the judges of the House of Lords, in deciding a case, ruled that certain sums received by a plaintiff by way of disability pension were not to be taken into account in calculating his damages.[22] So we have a rule made by Parliament and a rule made by the judges. In each instance, a law-making body has laid down a new rule which is to have general application to all similar cases that arise in the future. That is equally true of many rules laid down by the courts. Both Courts and Parliament are capable of creating, amending and repealing rules of quite general application. So let me illustrate how judges come to make law – bearing in mind that there are few areas in which judges are constitutionally incapable of making new law, though Parliament often tries to legislate unambiguously and comprehensively, leaving no gaps for the judges to fill. That has not proved easy.[23]

One branch of law extensively developed in hard-fought litigation over the last 150 years is that governing the rights to compensation of persons injured by the actions of others. The courts developed and applied the idea that certain people owed to other people particular duties. If those who owed the duties neglected to perform them and so caused injury to those to whom the duties were owed, the victims were entitled to recover monetary compensation from those whose neglect caused the injury. Thus the essential basis of the right to damages for personal injury was wrongdoing or fault – not fault in some abstract sense but fault consisting of breach of duty. So the courts had to decide if everybody owed duties to everybody else, or if there were limits. Were duties owed only by those who had, by entering into a contract, voluntarily entered into a relationship with others; or could there be duties apart altogether from contract? If an accident were brought about by several contributory causes, was the author of each cause responsible for the loss in whole, in part, or not at all? What if the victim himself were partly responsible? Should his fault, however small, absolve the other wrongdoers? Or should it simply reduce his right to compensation proportionately? Should people have to answer for the negligent acts of their servants? And what if the servants injured one another, was the master going to have to compensate a servant injured by the negligence of a fellow servant? Was the owner to be held liable for the damage done by his dog or his pet tiger? Was a proprietor to be held liable if dry rot spread from his house to an adjacent one, or his dam burst and flooded his neighbour's land? Well, of course, there are thousands of such questions. And it would have been an inconceivable effort of the imagination for lawyers, politicians, industrialists or anyone else to sit down and anticipate all the questions. What happened was that the courts waited until people brought contested claims and the resolution of each contest required the answering of the questions raised. Life after the Industrial Revolution – the growth of mechanical transport systems and the creation of huge urban working populations exposed to dangerous processes – was not slow in throwing up the questions. It might have been possible to try to enact codes of law from which the answers might be deducted. But that was not the way Victorian Britain faced up to the challenge of the new questions.

The British answer was to trust the judges. It was not so much a conscious decision as a default decision. And the judges were, as judges always are, creatures of their time, class and background, influenced and conditioned by their knowledge and their ignorance, their beliefs and their prejudices, intellectually indebted to Saint Paul and Adam Smith but not too familiar with mines, factories and docks. Thus equipped, they provided answers to whatever questions the cases put. People may talk about the edifice of the common law, but there was no grand design. It was erected a brick at a time. The doctrine of precedent saw to that. In so far as there were or were thought to be blueprints, they consisted of vague and imprecise notions, like the natural law or common sense. If there were conscious borrowings from developed and coherent systems, they were borrowings from old systems, such as the Roman law or the canon law, which had themselves evolved out of the experience and perceptions of different peoples, different times, different societies. And the principles and jurisprudential concepts that other societies had slowly fashioned were adapted to give some coherence to the developing system.[24]

Judges brought to the task a strong sense that, collectively, they were able to draw upon an infinite reservoir of natural law and right reason, of good custom and sound common sense. Their paths to that reservoir had been lighted by generations of wise men, mostly other judges, whose decisions and reasoning were to be accorded the highest respect. And the law, because of its origins and its antiquity, was perceived to be wiser than men, especially men who were not judges; and not just wiser but surer. Modern judges, unlike their predecessors, have had to learn to live with Parliament's inexhaustible drive to make and unmake law in all fields. But the traditions of the powerful, inspired judiciary endure. They have been seen from time to time in the judges' reluctance to give effect to legislation restricting common law rights.[25] They may be seen in the pleas to trust the judges.[26] In the last 35 years they have emerged strikingly in the judges' rediscovery of judiciary review.[27]

What the judges did was to resurrect and develop old forms of remedy to enable citizens to challenge infringements of their rights, especially infringements by public officials. This is the process known as judicial review of administrative action, or administrative review. Essentially, what the judges did was to turn their attention to a field in which they were the real experts: the field of remedies. They did not assert that they were creating new rights; they just claimed to be discovering ways of giving people access to rights which had lain unused because nobody could reach them. The judges did not stock the shelves; they merely unlocked the glass door behind which the rights sat, tantalisingly unobtainable. There were good historical precedents for proceeding in this undramatic fashion. Any lawyer appreciates that by providing ways of asserting rights, the judges have armed the citizen with rights that he did not know he had. Not only that; because once the rediscovered judicial tools for administrative review became known and widely used, the grounds for administrative review increased and multiplied. And government ministers and other public officials to whom Parliament had delegated wide power and discretion suddenly found that judges were once again prepared to police their use of power and discretion.

There is, no doubt, a long way to go yet, and it is possible to detect some unevenness in the readiness of judges to use their new jurisdiction. It is by no means easy to predict when the judges will step in and when they will stand back and decline to intervene. In one case, concerning the statutory guidance issued by the Secretary of State on local authorities' expenditure, the court declined to examine the detail of the guidance or its consequences, stating that it could do so only if it appeared that the Secretary of State had acted in bad faith or for an improper motive or had taken leave of his senses.[28] But in Mrs Gillick's case the same court made a most minute examination of guidance issued by the Department of Health and Social Security although no such suggestion was made.[29] On most occasions the court has explicitly confined itself to technical matters about how public officials have gone about exercising their responsibilities; but sometimes they have looked deeply into the factual basis of the decisions the officials have taken.[30] We see here echoes of the continuing debate that has exercised the United States Supreme Court for over a century, about the meaning of the words 'due process' in the 14th amendment. In some cases the courts have seemed to encourage those who seek judicial review of administrative action. But in a recent case the court expressed itself troubled at what was described as 'the prolific use of judicial review' to challenge the performance by local authorities of their functions under the Homeless Persons Act, 1977.[31] In some cases they have allowed attempts to challenge public administration to be choked by what the layman would see as technicalities.[32] In others, the technicalities have presented no insuperable obstacle.[33] So precisely how the courts will finally define the character and limits of their rediscovered jurisdiction is still uncertain. But its recent history illustrates that judges are still prepared to engage in what Lord Wilberforce described as cautious legislation,[34] even when, as its supporters claim, the judges are 'up to their necks in policy', and disobeying Acts of Parliament.[35] Most commentators credit the judges with being on the side of the angels, exercising what English judges see as their neglected but historical role of shielding the subject from attempts by the executive to encroach upon his liberty. It is also possible to interpret what is being done as signalling a rebellious stand against Parliamentary sovereignty, a move by the courts to reoccupy constitutional ground conceded by earlier generations of judges to the electorate.[36]

For judges to ensure that administrators stay within their statutory powers is one thing; to tell Parliament that it is abusing its sovereign power would be quite another. I believe that the underlying notion that our judges have a special gift for dispassionately applying a law older, wiser and surer than the laws that pour out of ever-changing Parliaments has led some to support the argument that there should be enacted an entrenched Bill of Rights, one which would enable the judiciary to engage in a wider judicial review, and strike down primary legislation if it failed to come up to the standards of the new natural law, as encapsulated in the Bill. So it is worth considering how the law made by judges compares with that made by elected Parliaments. And it is to that I shall turn next.

CHAPTER THREE

HARD CASES AND BAD LAW

•

In deciding the cases that come before them, judges can and do make law, and Parliament is free to accept that judge-made law or to alter it. If Parliament chooses to legislate, then, at least in theory, there can be no conflict between the law made by Parliament and the law applied in the courts. And if anyone wants to assert that the law made by Parliament is of an inferior metal, then the one audience that will not listen to that argument is the judiciary.[1]

But if we are to consider allowing the validity of laws enacted by Parliament to be challenged in the courts on the ground of supposed conflict with some fundamental or supreme law; if we are to think of allowing the judges' solutions, based upon their interpretation of an entrenched charter of fundamental law, to prevail over those of Parliament, then perhaps we ought first to give some thought to the character of law made by judges. I shall look at one field of law in which the courts were immensely creative and in which the judge-made law inevitably affected the lives of millions who had no part in the making of that law, little knowledge of its content, and no freedom to contract out of it: the field of law governing the rights of injured persons to recover damages in respect of accidental injury. Unlike many other areas of the law, such as those concerned with commercial contracts or wills, it was not practicable for most of the people affected by the law to study the judge-made rules with a view to modifying their behaviour so as to fit it within the rules.

The fundamental notion that judges developed to govern the making of reparation for accidental injury was the notion of wrong, of some fault, some blameworthiness on the part of an identified wrongdoer who could be made subject to the effective jurisdiction of the court and so be made to pay any damages found due. This is an individualistic and moralistic notion. It means that injury itself gives no right to compensation: the person who has done the injury must be identified and sued. The wrongdoer must be arraigned before the court, not to be punished but to be ordered to compensate in money.[2] The victim must obtain evidence to establish that the alleged wrongdoer has been guilty of a wrongful act which caused the injury. It is not enough that another's act has caused your injury. It has to be shown that that act was in breach of some duty that the law recognised as apt to create rights and obligations. Because there had to be proof by acceptable evidence of all the essentials, the victim had to have the economic capacity, and the will, to gather the evidence, to finance the litigation, to endure, if necessary, the extra legal sanctions that the alleged wrongdoer was free to deploy – such as the threat of dismissal from employment – as well as the capacity to wait, perhaps for years, for the case to be concluded. There was inevitably the risk of failure, but even an apparent success could sometimes be rendered hollow by the deduction of legal expenses incurred on the road to that success.

And there were other formidable obstacles. Contributory negligence, the judges decided, was a complete bar to success: and the employer was not held responsible when one employee negligently injured another; each employee was required to take the risk of his fellow servant's negligence, a judge-made doctrine which, though gradually modified, left a considerable gap in the rights of employed persons. Other claims were defeated by the development of the doctrine that certain people must be deemed to have voluntarily accepted risks to which they were exposed. And, by creating particular immunities, the judges erected other barriers to the recovery of compensation.[3] So the pursuit of compensation was a game of Snakes-and-Ladders, a lottery in which the innocence or the hurt of the victim was no guarantee of success. Some innocent victims recovered damages. Others did not. The chances of landing on a snake were so feared that even those who were able to make a substantial claim could seldom take the risk of a fight to the finish to obtain their whole rights. Most cases were compromised on the principle that a bird in the hand was worth three in the thicket.[4] And even with its successes, limited though they were, the judge-made law did little, if anything, to reduce the risk of injury. The courts could take no steps to attack the causes of industrial injury: it would have been difficult for judges so to develop their powers as to compel the introduction of safer working practices, to secure the performance of duty rather than just a payment for its breach.[5]

It would have been even more difficult for judges to develop a system whereby the payment of compensation depended on the need of the injured person rather than upon the responsibility of a wrongdoer; because litigation in the civil courts is concerned with vindicating the rights of one citizen at the expense of another. If the plaintiff wins damages it is because the defendant must pay them. The idea that a plaintiff could win a right to compensation without somebody's being held responsible to pay it just did not make sense in a court of law. Judges could not create a fund to enable compensation to be paid to those among the injured or bereaved who could not pin the blame upon a solvent wrongdoer. In a court, the idea of no-fault compensation was unthinkable. Judges could not reach out from the necessary limitations of the system in order to confer rights to compensation based solely upon need.

The judges who, over a long period of time, made such law, and then applied it, were certainly not operating in one of the law's unimportant backwaters. It was an area in which many people made their only contact with the law, and for many such people that contact was all-important. If the law allowed no redress for being blinded or crippled and gave no compensation, then they would look in vain elsewhere.

What are we to make of the body of law that the judges created? Though most people would agree that incoherence, illogicality and irrationality would be serious defects in the law, few would say that the law was good just because it was coherent, logical and based on a clear principle. Judges will very properly aim for these qualities. But in themselves, even when achieved, they do not make the law good. The law can be considered good only if, being coherent, predictable and principled, it also produces results which are socially acceptable. And the results of the judge-made law in the field of reparation for personal injury left too much to be desired. For too many there was, and is still, no remedy.

For those for whom the law could provide a remedy, the route to it was slow, expensive, hazardous and uncertain. Even from the defendant's point of view, the law was unsatisfactory. The cost of litigation was high. Insuring against the risks of litigation became very high. It has recently become clear – especially in America, where generally[6] the same legal principles apply – that the fear of being sued, and the cost of insuring against that risk, have begun to make serious inroads into the availability of vital public services, including medical treatment.[7] When the law, properly applied, produces the result that those who need medical treatment cannot have it because doctors are afraid of being sued, then it produces a result which is not socially acceptable.

If we end up, as we do, with a body of law which affords remedies which too often have the appearance of tickets in a lottery,[8] which threatens to inhibit the provision of medical care or other necessary services and which hardly serves to raise standards of care, then it is little wonder that some countries have decided to abandon the whole judge-made edifice and introduce no-fault compensation.[9]

It would be wrong to suggest that there was no rhyme or reason to it all; there was. It was not necessarily the logic of the judges that was to blame; it was the major premises that preceded the adjudication. And quite apart from the constitutional inability of our courts to reach out and introduce positive measures designed to achieve social justice, the very nature of litigation and of judicial training are such that judges cannot calculate or control the long-term effects of the law, which they build up painstakingly, one decision at a time.

In the United States Supreme Court, judges can, and do, select and assemble a whole spectrum of real cases to be considered at the one time and can hear representations not just from the interested parties but from others who are concerned about the consequence for the law of whatever ruling is made.[10] So the judges obtain briefings about the social and economic results of formulating the law in a particular way before deciding what the policy of the law is to be. But once judges do that, they have ceased to be judges as we know them. They have become legislators making informed policy choices. I do not believe that our judges can or should be given such tools, or such a role. It is not a role which, by tradition, training or experience they are qualified to perform. When we ask judges to decide the legal rights and wrongs of litigants we are doing something for which there is no tenable alternative. Someone must resolve the disputes. It has to be judges. And there is no escape from using, as judges, lawyers whose mental equipment includes assumptions and prejudgments which lie outside the letter of the law. Equally, we have to accept that, as they decide one case after another, some of these very assumptions and prejudgments become part of the law, as much, indeed, as if they had been enacted by Parliament.

In a common-law tradition like ours, the judges have to fill the gaps and make law. But let us be clear that this is what they are doing. Let us understand that society, if it does not review the provisional, the necessary, the imperfect law made by judges, is abdicating the making of its policy choices to what Lord Devlin called 'a body of elderly men'.[11] It is the proper function of governments and democratically elected legislators to consider and make policy choices, not the proper function of judges.

That in itself is no startling or revolutionary proposition. On the contrary, it has been accepted in modern times that an activist Parliament must intervene in order to remake or restate the law which has been evolved by judges. And Parliament must fulfil that role not just when the whole thrust of the judge-made law has produced results which are notoriously seen to be no longer socially acceptable. It must do so at all times to grapple with the classic problem of law in society; the difficulty, some would say the impossibility, of writing down the law so that it is certain and its application predictable, while at the same time ensuring that it prescribes and achieves a fair and just result in individual cases. It is, for the most part, the courts, the judges, that have to resolve the so-called 'hard cases', the cases in which the law points to a result which appears to be unfair, or the cases in which different principles or rules of law clash and compel a choice, a choice which determines the result.[12] This problem can, of course, arise whether the existing law has been enacted by Parliament or created by judges. It will commonly arise if, when the law was laid down, the particular problem was not foreseen, perhaps because it could not have been foreseen. Thus, for example, the law which defined adultery and held it to be a matrimonial offence, giving rise to certain rights in the innocent spouse, had settled down and appeared to be comprehensively defined and understood, until science discovered a way of impregnating a woman artificially with the semen of a man whom she had never met. Until then the law was quite simple. If a man had lived completely apart from his wife for a year and then discovered she was pregnant he could divorce her on the ground of adultery; the law would hold the pregnancy to be sufficient evidence of adultery, and there could be no answer. Then science provided an answer. The wife, in a particular case, could say: 'I haven't committed adultery; I have been made pregnant by artificial insemination.'[13] Today, she might go further and say: 'I have hired out my womb for a fee and am merely a host for someone else's fertilised ovum.' So, for the first time, lawyers have to decide if physical intercourse is the essential feature of adultery, or whether adultery is committed when a wife conceives a child of which her husband is not the father.

A judge faced with such a question cannot sidestep it by saying: 'This is an unforeseen and unprovided-for situation; let Parliament deal with it.' He has to decide,[14] and some new law is made. Obviously, most advances in technology are capable of throwing up unforeseen problems for which the existing law does not provide and the old law has to be stretched by judges to furnish answers which will fill the gaps until Parliament attempts to fashion a legal structure to regulate the rights and responsibilities of those affected by the new state of facts. But even without the trigger of technological innovation, gradual changes in the perception of what is fair and reasonable can suggest that the old law is inadequate, and cause judges to nurture new principles and limit old ones in order to impose restrictions or make available remedies that were not available before. This happened in relation to the concept of cruelty in matrimonial cases, in which the judges gradually departed from the idea that such cruelty had to be physical, and allowed divorce for mental cruelty.[15] Likewise, in the field of public order, the courts responded to unwelcomed forms of protest by adapting the concept of breach of the peace.[16] And the unfairness of the judge-made doctrine of common employment led later judges to modify its excesses, though, until Parliament intervened, the law remained unjust.[17]

The so-called 'hard cases' in which the justice of the case leads to one result, though the existing law points to another, do not always produce bad law in the sense that the particular results are unfair; but they tend to produce uncertain law. Law which is uncertain is bad in principle, even if the results in particular cases can be justified. When long-standing rules can be abandoned, when too many cases divide judicial opinion and can be decided either way, then the warning signals should be out.

Yet despite the wisdom of the judges, despite their independence, despite their impartiality, their traditions, their analytical skills, they disagree about what the law is or should be. Such disagreement is unlikely to flow from overt political preferences. It flows from the fact that where there is uncertainty, there is bound to be disagreement. Unanimity is a rare phenomenon when there is room for doubt. And the law, even today, contains a surprisingly large number of grey areas.

That is true even in the criminal law: the recent report of the Fraud Trials Committee,[18] sitting under the chairmanship of Lord Roskill, illustrates that even an apparently simple concept like dishonesty is one that the law and judges, at least in England, cannot readily explain to juries. A recent well-known case demonstrates a similar phenomenon. The case is *R* v. *Hancock and Another*,[19] the case of the two striking Welsh miners who killed a taxi driver by dropping concrete on his taxi as he drove another miner to work. The facts were simple enough, but the critical question was whether the two miners had acted with what the law would recognise as murderous intent. That looks like a question of fact. But the trial judge explained the law about intent in such terms that after some five hours the jury sent a note to the judge indicating that they were perplexed. So the judge gave them further directions in law. If they were puzzled the first time, the second direction would not have helped them, because the trial judge just repeated to the jury what he had said the first time.[20] That is hardly surprising, because he was being extremely careful to give the jury exactly the directions which had been prescribed by the House of Lords itself only a short time before in the case of *Maloney*. The jury brought in a verdict of murder against the two miners. On appeal, the Court of Appeal quashed the conviction for murder and substituted a verdict of manslaughter. They did so on the ground that what the trial judge had said was potentially misleading: in other words, that the House of Lords had got it wrong in the earlier (*Maloney*)[21] case.

So the Crown appealed to the Lords, who had then to decide if the guidelines they had laid down in *Maloney's* case were sound or defective. They agreed that the guidelines laid down in *Maloney's* case were defective, but they disagreed with the Court of Appeal's suggestions as to what the guidelines ought to be in future cases. Exactly where that leaves the trial judge in future cases has yet to be seen. But it must be a matter for some dismay that in 1985 and 1986 the judges in the highest courts were still at sixes and sevens as to the appropriate formulation of the guidance to be given to juries on a matter as basic, as common and as elementary as intent in a murder case. There is something wrong when, after considering hundreds of criminal cases involving intent, we still cannot produce an agreed and universally accepted statement of precisely what the law requires for proof of specific intent.

No one can criticise the jury in the *Hancock* case. There is a tendency, which is by no means new, to claim that juries cannot be trusted to handle complex criminal cases. But if the *Hancock* saga is evidence of anything, it is that the problem is not in the jury but in the remarkable difficulty that judges have in determining and explaining the legal principles and rules which juries have to apply.

The inevitable result of reducing the role of the jury would be to increase the role of the judge. So it is worth glancing at the other half of that remarkable forensic partnership.

The jury is not one unvarying institution, possessing the same character and powers wherever it is found. Juries vary in size from six to 15 members.[22] They decide civil and criminal cases. Sometimes they have to be unanimous.[23] Sometimes they are allowed to deliver a verdict by a simple[24] or a qualified[25] majority. They mostly resolve issues of fact, but sometimes must decide mixed questions of fact and law. In some jurisdictions they may have a role in the sentencing process, as well as in determining guilt or innocence.[26] And the nature of the right to a jury trial in a criminal case varies in different countries. I have no wish to provide an index to all varieties of the jury. It would be substantial. I merely want to caution against the insular notion that the jury is an institution as unvarying in time and character as the Rock of Ages. It is not, even when it is embedded, as in America, in a constitution. It is a tool with many different uses and dimensions.

The use of juries has had a profound effect upon court procedures and rules of evidence. Juries came to cases totally ignorant of the background; some jurors could not read.[27] So the trial took the form of an oral presentation of the facts, with both sides having carefully defined rights to present and to challenge evidence before an open-minded court. Neither judge nor jury had an inquisitorial role. The rules of evidence were fashioned to ensure that juries heard nothing that might prejudice their consideration of the narrow issues they had to resolve, and the jury sat mute until it pronounced the winners and the losers.

Learned commentators, here and in America, compared the form of litigation resulting from the use of juries to a sporting contest,[28] a boxing match, a fox-hunt.[29] Lord Devlin expressed the more traditional view in describing the criminal jury system as 'the lamp of freedom . . . the beacon that seven centuries have tended'.[30] Lord Denning said it was 'the best guarantee of our freedoms[31] I agree with that. But it is best to see the jury as it is: an imperfect instrument in an imperfect world, an instrument fashioned by history, rather than by any very conscious design, an instrument that takes on a local colour in different jurisdictions.[32]

So what are we to make of Lord Devlin's assertion that if there were a tyrant in Whitehall his first object would be to make Parliament utterly subservient to his will, and the next to overthrow or diminish trial by jury? Since he spoke, the Diplock courts have replaced jury trials in Northern Ireland in relation to offences from murder downwards[33] and, after public calls by some judges, the Fraud Trials Committee, under the chairmanship of Lord Roskill, has proposed that for certain fraud cases trial by tribunal should replace trial by jury.[34] These and other changes certainly diminish trial by jury.[35] So are there tyrants in Whitehall? I hope not. I think it is going too far to suggest that simply altering the jury system is necessarily a giant leap towards tyranny. If it were, then Scotland – where there is no automatic right to a jury trial in most cases, and where juries can return a verdict by a simple majority – must have been in the grip of tyrants for centuries.[36]

Too many lawyers take a patronising view of juries.[37] For myself, I have prosecuted and defended in complex fraud, corruption and other such trials in Scotland, with jurors selected from the voters' roll, with some of the jurors almost as young as the accused in the dock and some almost as old as the judge on the bench, without ever feeling that the jury failed to understand by the end what the point was. We should not patronise jurors by regarding them as too young, too old, too immature or too stupid to understand how an accused person has brought about some definite practical result by false pretences.[38] If it really were true that jurors could not, after hearing the evidence, understand the types of fraud case listed in the Roskill report then they really have no business to be deciding about murder, rape and arson.[39] If there is something wrong with the way in which those who perpetrate frauds are brought to justice, or are not brought to justice, then the probability is that those who investigate such frauds are not up to the task and those who present the cases to the jury are unable to see the wood for the trees.

I am not persuaded that the system for establishing the guilt or innocence of those charged with complex fraud or any other serious crime has broken down. If it is showing signs of stress then I consider that those who lay the blame on the jury are firing at the wrong target. If we are to trim the wick of the lamp of freedom, let us do it on the basis of evidence that it is necessary, not just because some people suppose that judges could make a better job of determining guilt or innocence than a large body of properly instructed citizens sitting as jurors. What has to be done is to simplify the law, to improve the facilities for juries, to humanise court rituals and modernise rules of evidence, and to devise ways to ensure that the cases are presented to juries in a manner that is worthy of the high intellectual competence and substantial remuneration of the lawyers, including judges, who take part in such trials.

Of course juries sometimes acquit people who probably have committed the crimes with which they have been charged. But the principal reason for that is that under our law no person can be convicted of a crime unless his guilt is established beyond reasonable doubt, upon the basis of admissible evidence. I would not for one moment suggest that we should tamper with the burden or the standard of proof. I ask merely that we acknowledge that it is that standard, and not the gullibility of jurors, that secures acquittals in most of those cases in which the prosecution fails. If it happens too often that the guilty go free, let us rather re-examine the rules and procedures, to see if in a civilised society we can properly provide the jury with more pieces of the jigsaw of truth.

I am not sure if the current criticisms of the criminal jury system and how it is seen to operate spring from the same attitudes that cause some lawyers to wax lyrical about the new activism of judges in judicial review and urge the dramatic change in the scope and character of judicial review that enacting a Bill of Rights would effect. Certainly, diminishing the role of the jury while enlarging that of the judge would achieve a significant shift of power in the whole field of public order. And obviously, to diminish the system of trial by jury and at the same time to enact a Bill of Rights is to engage judges in highly visible activities, all related to law, order, justice and freedom.

What I question is the true relevance of such changes to the real problems of order and justice. To enact a Bill of Rights in noble language and to set judges to apply it to cases would, I suspect, be the modern equivalent of writing and producing a morality play. It would be entertaining, even instructive, and would allow us to applaud the occasional triumph of those values that the scriptwriters favoured. But it would have little effect on how people behaved in the real world.

CHAPTER FOUR

TRUSTING THE JUDGES

•

In the law, avoidable uncertainty is an evil, and unfettered judicial freedom of choice a vice. Consider, for example, how the law applies to industrial relations. The law must apply in some shape or form, because the law cannot be absent from this, or, indeed, from any other area of social activity. Even if Parliament were to pass an Act saying, 'All laws applying to trade unions are thereby repealed', that itself would be creating a complex legal status for trade unions: a status which, with its privileges and immunities, the courts would have to take account of if anyone raised an action against a body which claimed to be a trade union. Indeed the new law would obviously have to define what a trade union was for the purposes of its application. Even though the existing law or the ordinary law could be disapplied, the result would be to create by law a particular set of rights and immunities for any body successfully claiming to be a trade union. So it is axiomatic that some law has to apply in the field of industrial relations, whether it is intrusive and regulatory or restrained and permissive.

Is it not plain that the law that does apply, whatever it may say, should be precise in its statement, certain in its effect and therefore predictable in its consequences? Neither those in industry, nor their customers, nor the public at large can afford to wait for years or even months while the legal aspects of industrial disputes are debated through the courts at the stately pace of the Jarndyce litigation in Dickens's *Bleak House* – but with the predictability of the Grand National. Nor, indeed, can society readily accept a situation in which, because the answers are uncertain, the courts have to pronounce what are said to be temporary orders but which, because of the nature of the matter involved and the law's delays, in effect determine decisively the legal rights of the parties.[1]

In the law, as in much of the rest of life, we make people abide by the rules. But that is tolerable only if people can readily discover what the rules are and what they mean. The law is fair only if it is precise. That is why, at the price of inelegant complexity, our Acts of Parliament endeavour to spell out with mathematical precision what the rules are.

From the judges' point of view, uncertainty creates another danger. If the application of the law be left uncertain, if policy choices have to be made, if there are respectable legal routes leading in opposite directions, then the judges (who have to choose one route or the other) will inevitably, and correctly, be accused of making choices upon grounds other than purely legal ones. And the courts will be dragged into politics. It has happened before. Everyone agrees that judges should stay out of politics, even if people don't try to spell out the reasons for that very clearly. I suppose they must include the fact that judges, by reason of age, sex and background, might find it difficult to appear impartial and could never hope to be representative or accountable. But I need not discuss this because the principle is not in dispute. From a strictly judicial viewpoint, it matters relatively little what the law provides; what matters is that it be clear and unambiguous.[2]

That is true not just of industrial relations but of religious and moral questions, like abortion, contraception and the right to die; and socio-political questions, like positive discrimination or the balance between civil rights and the investigative powers of the police. It is inevitable that the courts will be called upon to adjudicate in cases in which such matters are in dispute, because access to the courts is a fundamental feature of the rule of law. But the method of adjudication ought, as far as possible, to be the relatively mechanical process of applying a precise set of unambiguous rules to the facts, not a wide-ranging philosophical exercise in making policy choices.

The greater the latitude allowed to judges, the greater is the risk of their appearing arbitrary, capricious and biased. In the 'hard' cases – those in which, because the law is ambiguous or silent, judges frequently disagree both as to the law and the result – the choice of result, the formulation of the law is in truth a policy choice.[3] Sometimes the judge will consciously make, and declare that he is making, a policy choice. Sometimes the judge will present it as a legal choice, compelled inexorably by the application of sound principles and authoritative precedents; he will emerge from the delivery-room declaring that the newborn rule is legitimate but claiming that he is merely a midwife, not the parent. But, in one sense, it hardly matters who claims paternity for the new law. For it has become an independent entity with a life of its own. It is the law. And it will remain the law until somebody alters it.

If a higher court cannot or will not alter it, it can be altered only by Parliament. If Parliament thinks about the rightness and wisdom of that piece of law, it is not bound or shackled by inherited legal principle or precedent. Parliament avowedly looks at the policy choice and asks: should the law remain in the state fashioned by the judges or should it be changed? And Parliament, if it is doing its job properly, examines the social and economic justifications for altering the law or leaving it as it is. Lord Denning, when delivering the 1980 Richard Dimbleby lecture, exhorted us to trust the judges. Well, of course we can trust the judges. We can trust them not to fiddle the results. We can trust them to apply the law honestly to the case. We can trust them from time to time to discover and enunciate new or revised rules of law. We can trust them to make the difficult choices. We can even trust them – if only because there is no alternative – to make interim policy choices about what the law should be, if such choices have not already been made by the legislature. But there is no sound reason for trusting judges to make final policy choices. Final policy choices fall to be made by society as a whole, not by lawyers, however distinguished and upright they may be.

So if judges choose that contributory negligence or common employment is to be a complete bar to recovering damages for personal injury, society does not have to accept that as a final, unreviewable choice written on tablets of stone. Society can say (as it did on both these points), thank you, but if that is the law, the law is an ass. Society can and should choose to reject judge-made law when its social results are unacceptable. Trust the judges to plant the tree and till the soil. But if the fruit be sour, graft on a new strain or chop down the tree. And that is exactly what, as a society, we have always retained an unfettered right to do when judge-made solutions were or became unacceptable or seemed to produce injustice. The point about the development of the law in our society is that the lawgivers, whether they are judges or legislators, create general rules intended to yield acceptable results in all foreseeable cases. Then life throws up unforeseen cases, and either they or changes in society's perceptions show that the rules are inadequate. So they are changed. The courts are the laboratory in which the rules are tested against reality and proved for social justice. We can trust the judges to do that.

But we should not trust them to write and to rewrite the rules; because the judicial system has a powerful constitutional inertia which resists change, because judges baulk at changing the settled law, because judges cannot reach out and create whole new systems of law, because courts are not equipped to assess the social merits of law reform and because judges are not the right people to make the necessary value-judgments. So, to face up to Lord Denning's invitation to trust the judges: the correct riposte is, trust them to do what? If the invitation is to trust them to make enduring policy changes, I suggest we don't. The cobbler should stick to his last. The judge should be confined to resolving disputes by applying the law. Lawmaking should be left to lawmakers, policymaking to responsible policy-makers.

And that's just the problem with a constitutional Bill of Rights. It is inevitably a charter of enduring super-rights, rights written in delphic words but in indelible ink on an opaque surface. It turns judges into legislators and gives them a finality which our whole tradition has hitherto professed to withhold from them. It makes the mistake of dressing up policy choices as if they were legal choices. It asks those whose jobs it is to know and apply the law to create and reform the law. It requires those whose skill it is to know what the law is to decide what it should be. If the legislature shirks the task of deciding what the law should be, either by avoiding the issue altogether, as it sometimes does, or by addressing the issue but refusing to make the essential detailed policy choices, the judges are compelled to step into the breach. Judges abhor a legal vacuum. So if legislators or constitution-makers pronounce resoundingly that 'All men are equal' but fail to indicate whether 'men' includes or excludes women, slaves, blacks, aliens or unborn foetuses or corporate persons, then judges have to decide. The decision cannot be made on the basis of the words alone: words, as Humpty Dumpty reminded us, mean whatever we say they mean. If legislators don't tell us precisely what the words mean, then the words will mean what the judges say they mean.[4]

The words which were put into the Constitution of the United States, and into the Bill of Rights which became part of the Constitution, left many vital questions unanswered. Precisely why some questions were left unanswered is an historical matter. But no doubt some were avoided because there was no political consensus as to what the answers should be. Others were not thought about because in the prevailing social climate the questions did not arise. Others were unforeseeable because the technological advances which later posed the questions had not yet occurred.[5] The 18th century Americans, although they provided mechanisms for constitutional amendments, did not make it clear exactly how the unresolved questions were to be answered in the absence of any such amendment; but within 20 years, the judges, under the leadership of Chief Justice Marshall, were claiming – and were eventually accorded – the responsibility for providing the answers, upon the theory that they were somehow bringing to light answers that lay beneath the written word.[6]

In the result, the Supreme Court of the United States became and has remained a dignified cauldron in which the essentially political questions of race, civil liberties, economic regulation, abortion, contraception, freedom of speech, pornography, capital punishment and the powers of the President have been debated by lawyers and decided by lawyers. Alexis de Tocqueville's observation, 150 years ago, that 'scarcely any political question arises in the United States that is not resolved, sooner or later, into a judicial question', could be echoed by Daniel Boorstin in 1955. 'The Supreme Court,' he wrote, 'has become the American political conscience, a kind of secular papacy, a new search in every generation for what the more large-minded and more foresighted of the Founders might have meant if they were alive. All the crises in our political history have sooner or later been stated in legal terms.'[7]

Those who interpret a constitution cannot avoid choosing among competing social and political visions. The walls between the political and judicial systems become paper-thin. Just think about the kind of political and social questions that American judges have been asked to resolve. They have had to decide if telephones could lawfully be tapped,[8] if the mentally subnormal could be compulsorily sterilised,[9] if minimum-wages laws could be enacted,[10] if blacks and white could intermarry,[11] if capital punishment were permitted by the Constitution,[12] if married couples could lawfully use contraceptive devices,[13] if the President was subject to the law,[14] if abortion was prohibited by the Constitution,[15] how electoral boundaries should be drawn,[16] whether schoolchildren had to salute the American flag,[17] whether the races should be segregated on trains[18] and in schools,[19] whether women could be barred from practising the law,[20] what powers the police could exercise in investigating crime.

Let us look in just a little more detail at two cases concerning police powers. The first is the case of *Miranda*.[21] Ernesto Miranda was arrested at his home and taken to a Phoenix police station, where he was accused of kidnapping and rape. After being identified by the complaining witness, he was questioned by two policemen in a secluded room for two hours. He was not told of his right not to be compelled to incriminate himself. At the end of the interrogation, he signed a typewritten confession prepared by the police. On that evidence he was convicted. The question before the Supreme Court of the United States was whether the obtaining of a self-incriminating confession by such methods violated Mr Miranda's constitutional rights; and, if so, whether the evidence of the confession should have been allowed to be heard at the trial. In considering how to apply the Constitution to the case, the justices looked at their legal history in such matters. By the end of the 18th century, the American colonists had a profound and sharpened awareness of the injustices perpetrated in the English state trials and in Continental Europe by odious and cruel methods of interrogating accused or suspected persons to force confessions from them. So deeply did the iniquities of the ancient systems impress themselves upon the minds of those who enacted the American Bill of Rights that they made the rule against such confessions not merely a rule of evidence, as in England or Scotland, but a part of their fundamental law, 'clothed with the impregnability of a constitutional enactment'. They enacted the Fifth Amendment, which provides that no person shall be compelled in any criminal case to be a witness against himself.

By 1966, when Ernesto Miranda's case came before it, the Supreme Court had, in a series of earlier cases, already rejected evidence improperly extracted by the police use of so-called 'third-degree' methods, both physical and psychological. So when Miranda's case came before it, the court decided that persons who had been interrogated in police premises, cut off from the outside world, not told of their right to remain silent or told of their right to have a lawyer present, such persons had been deprived of their constitutional rights; and that confessions obtained by such interrogations should not be accepted as evidence by the courts. The courts, while acknowledging that the legislators had the right to find ways to give those who were detained by the police the protection which the Constitution accorded, prescribed safeguards which had to be observed, and laid down concrete constitutional guidelines for law-enforcement agencies and courts. Miranda's conviction was quashed.

Let me look next at another civil liberties case, *Mapp* v. *Ohio*.[22] On May 23, 1957, three Cleveland police officers arrived at Miss Mapp's house, looking for a person whom they wished to question about a recent bombing. They apparently had information that he was hiding in the house and that there might be hidden there a large amount of what was described as 'policy paraphernalia'. The police had no search-warrant, and Miss Mapp, after taking legal advice, refused to admit them. Three hours later, several policemen forced the door of the flat. Miss Mapp's attorney had arrived by this time but the police kept him out of the house and would not let him see his client, who, incidentally, was not accused of any crime. She asked to see their search-warrant. They didn't have one. But one officer held up a piece of paper claiming it was a warrant. Miss Mapp seized it and placed it in her bosom from where the officers recovered it, after a struggle. They then overpowered and handcuffed the lady because she had been, they said, 'belligerent' in resisting the recovery of the supposed warrant. Next, they searched the entire premises. They found no bomber and no policy paraphernalia, but they found some literature which they considered to be obscene. They took possession of it without her consent, and she was charged on an obscenity charge. The evidence against her on the obscenity charge was illegally obtained in violation of Miss Mapp's fundamental constitutional right: the right not to be subjected to unreasonable searches. But the illegally obtained evidence was allowed in at the trial and she was convicted on the obscenity charge and sentenced to imprisonment. The Supreme Court, by five to four, decided that the evidence obtained by the unconstitutional search was inadmissible, and the conviction was quashed.

It is of some interest to know that the Scottish courts, at least in 1957, and without reference to any entrenched constitutional rights would have arrived at the same result as did the majority of the Supreme Court. The evidence would have been excluded for the same basic reason, namely that the only practicable way the courts can curb the abuse of power by the police is to exclude evidence improperly obtained by such abuse. In other words, the courts will not sanction the use of grossly illegal means by the police to discover or prove illegal activities by the citizens.[23]

Now it is clear that rules that prevent the court from hearing evidence because of disapproval of the way in which it has been obtained can result in the acquittal of the guilty. Society must strike a reasonable balance between excluding improperly obtained evidence on the one hand, and acquitting guilty men on the other. The trouble with doing it by excluding relevant and convincing evidence, on the basis that some kinds of search amount to a violation of a constitutional right, means that society cannot readily adjust on any principled basis the delicate balance between the interests of society in safe-guarding civil liberties and the interests of justice in convicting the guilty. Yet situations may arise, for example in relation to the conduct of organised crime or the trafficking in dangerous drugs, in which the balance has to be swiftly and radically readjusted.[24] So the Americans, in order to adjust the balance, have either to amend the Constitution or to overrule or sidestep the decisions of the Supreme Court in such cases as *Miranda* and *Mapp*.[25] In the United Kingdom, by contrast, the general rule can be altered by an Act of Parliament, or particular rules can be introduced for particular cases.[26]

In the United States, the exclusionary rule, as it is called (seen at work in the cases I have described), has become the symbol of a wide-ranging battle in which different interests argue about police powers and civil liberties, about law and order and about the role of the courts. It necessarily becomes tied up with broader issues, such as the responsibility and answerability of the judges, the intentions of the constitution-makers, the boundaries between states' rights and federal rights, and the means which society can adopt to fight any crime wave which is seen as likely to pose a serious threat to that society. It is, of course, extremely important to strike a just balance between the freedom of law-enforcement agencies to investigate crime effectively and the necessary liberties of the subject. But this balance is not, I believe, a balance that can be struck once and for all time, and for all cases. Indeed, there is no need for it to be. Most citizens are willing to concede substantial restrictions upon their civil liberties when they see their society threatened by some great and imminent danger, for example in time of war, or when terrorists are perpetrating outrages, of if the country is facing a great and growing problems of hard-drug abuse or organised crime.

For it is not only in wartime that the community might think it necessary to resort to measures to protect itself against a frightening threat; only to find that such measures may be prohibited by its written constitution. The threat posed by the circulation of hard drugs is one that might call for measures such as mandatory testing which would be inconsistent with traditional constitutional safeguards as interpreted by the courts in quite different situations. The rapid spead of AIDS is another. It has been described in one American court, with some exaggeration, as the modern-day equivalent of leprosy. In different parts of the United States, regulations have been made empowering health officials to close bathhouses and massage parlours used by homosexual men; other regulations deny certain jobs to AIDS patients or bar children with AIDS from schools. Some proposals have been made to put AIDS patients in quarantine, or to make blood-testing compulsory, to discriminate against AIDS patients in housing and medical treatment.[27] Similar proposals have been made here. Such measures are already being challenged in American courts because they interfere with the rights of citizens who are innocent members of a class of persons afflicted by a disease for which they bear no responsibility.

But if the elected legislature and public health authorities conclude, on the basis of evidence, that such measures are necessary to limit the spead of this new and frightening disease to others, should their judgment be subject to veto by a court of law on the basis that the measures proposed to infringe rights conferred by a 200-year-old Bill of Rights? It is not an easy question to answer; but I suspect the public would prefer that such decisions be taken by elected bodies which are answerable directly to the public, not by courts which are not.

Quite apart from special or sudden threats, most citizens concerned about the general increase in reported crime would appear to consider it sensible to increase police powers at the expense of certain of the citizens' freedoms. And, whatever reservations one might have about particular proposals, the right way to do it is surely to allow the law to be altered by Parliament to try to meet the present dangers and to be free to do so in the light of our contemporary perception of the contemporary problem, not restricted by forms of words written at a different time in different circumstances and interpreted by lawyers who cannot be called to account.

Neither system ensures a perfect balancing in all circumstances, but in this kind of area, as in many others, flexibility, speed of response, and sensibility to what society wants or will put up with, are benefits that are more readily obtainable without the constraint of an entrenched body of constitutional law, enshrined in binding decisions of the highest court in the land.

If the creation, development and reform of the law which governs the admissibility of evidence in criminal trials, and in consequence regulates what the law-enforcement agencies may or may not do, if this is left to judges, then the side-effects of their lawmaking may prove to be serious and harmful. Obviously if the law so created, developed and applied begins to produce results which, in practice, impede the enforcement of the criminal law, then the judges, like most others, will want to see it changed. But the only way that judges can change the law which they themselves have created is to overrule their previous decisions or to find sophisticated ways of sidestepping them.[28]

The principal way of avoiding being bound by a precedent without going the length of overruling it, is to 'distinguish' it: to discover in the previous case some specialty, often of fact, which enables the judges to say that it has laid down no general rule.[29] Judges are not always reticent about the exercise of this forensic skill. So we have Lord Denning, while still Master of the Rolls, telling the Upper House of Parliament about how the Court of Appeal sidestepped the civil law governing some aspects of the law of contract.[30] What he said was: 'That was the law as laid down in 1934, and it has remained so ever since. However, I shall tell your Lordships how we got round it.'; adding: 'We in the Court of Appeal have ways of getting round things.' Judges are not always as frank. But once judges start getting round the law, not only do they create uncertainty – which itself necessarily creates injustice – but they threaten to undermine the whole traditional and constitutional basis of the authority of the judiciary.

The basis of that authority is not the wisdom or sense of justice or the charisma of particular judges. The true basis is that described by a great American judge, Learned Hand: 'His authority and immunity depend upon the assumption that he speaks from the mouth of others, he must present his authority by cloaking himself in the majesty of an overshadowing past.'[31] When judges start to get round the law – whether they throw off disguises and do it openly, or pay mere lipservice to the law that their predecessors have laid down – they set a destructive example for all for whom the established law has become an inconvenience. Few today would accuse British judges of dissembling and using the words they have inherited to impose their own subjective notions on contemporary society. But do we want to encourage or to drive the judiciary into fashioning enduring rights and duties from the interplay of their subjective notions of social justice and the words of some text that accords to them a wide freedom of choice? I suggest we do not.

CHAPTER FIVE

AN ENORMOUS POWER

•

Though it is clear that there are wider arguments about the wisdom of enacting an enduring constitutional document containing a selection of rights, intended to be overriding or fundamental, my principal purpose is to consider the effect of such a step upon the rôle of the judiciary, and indeed upon the law itself. In doing so I should make clear my belief that, although the historical, legal and constitutional differences between the United States and the United Kingdom are considerable, there are some lessons that we can learn from American experience that we cannot learn anywhere else.

But, before I attempt to show why that is so, let me remind you that the essential constitutional difference between our higher judicial system and that of the United States is that American judges are the guardians and interpreters of a written constitution. That constitution, containing the Bill of Rights, has long been regarded as a living source of philosophy and principle. It contains the text of a supreme law which provides the legal warrant for judges to make enduring social and political choices. By contrast, our judges, whatever the social or political implications of their lawmaking, are in no sense the final arbiters of such choices. Whatever law they create is at the immediate disposal of Parliament. The mistakes our judges make are not woven into the fabric of a supreme law beyond the reach of the legislature. The same applies to their achievements. Their finest works are, at least in theory, able to be swept away by a sovereign Parliament. This perception of the theoretical vulnerability both of the law's treasury of individual rights and of our essential constitutional machinery has led some to advocate a new constitutional settlement, designed and constructed to be proof against being dismantled by a temporary elected majority. A vital ingredient of such a settlement would be a statement of selected basic rights. If I am right in believing that such a change would make our judges perform tasks for which they are not equipped, and risk drawing them into the political arena in a way alien to the best traditions of the judiciary, we must before embarking upon it be satisfied that the change is reasonably necessary. As Murphy's law says: 'If a thing ain't broke, don't fix it.'

The countries which have inherited the Common Law tradition and which also practise multi-party representative democracy have, for the most part, managed hitherto to do without entrenched Bills of Rights. Canada's Charter of Rights and Freedoms was brought into force in April 1982 by an Act passed by the Westminster Parliament.[1] But section 15, the important provision relating to equality rights, did not come into effect until April 1985.[2] Quebec has exercised its right to disapply important parts of the Charter. In the first four years, the Supreme Court of Canada heard argument in just over 30 Charter cases and delivered judgment in 13. Arguments based on Charter Rights have, of course, been advanced in many hundreds of cases, mostly criminal, in lower courts; but, until the Supreme Court of Canada has decided many more Charter cases, it will be impossible to assess its real impact upon the law, or upon the role of the judges. So it is still too early to assess the accuracy of one senator's prediction that the Charter would provide a 'field-day for crackpots, a pain in the neck for judges and legislators and a goldmine for lawyers'.[3] But it is already possible to see that it is adding materially to the caseload of the courts and the workload of lawyers. Or, to put it another way, it is adding to the delay, the cost and the uncertainty of litigation.

In New Zealand, the Bill of Rights debate began in the 1960s. In 1985 the Minister of Justice presented to the House of Representatives a White Paper containing a draft Bill of Rights for New Zealand. The draft Bill owes much to the Canadian Charter; it draws heavily upon the experience of Canada and the United States. The first point that strikes the United Kingdom observer is that New Zealand has no second House of Parliament to act as a check upon the elected House of Representatives. So if that House, while under the control of an elected majority, chose to pass legislation which abolished or overrode the constitutional conventions – for example, by prolonging the life of that elected chamber without the inconvenience of having to face the electorate in a general election – there would be no proven and effective mechanisms to prevent it. And equally, it would be able, in theory, to make massive inroads into civil and human rights. The powers of the Governor-General or the courts of New Zealand to restrain such actions are, it is said, untested and uncertain, and might well prove to be ineffectual. This argument resembles Lord Hailsham's assertion, made about the British House of Commons, that it can be an 'instrument of tyranny'.[4] The point may be theoretically sound for the House of Representatives in New Zealand, though not for the British House of Commons, which cannot abolish the

House of Lords. But this much is clear; that in New Zealand the Bill of Rights argument is closely bound up with the argument that the country needs a constitution which cannot be dismantled by an executive commanding an absolute majority in a sovereign unicameral legislature. In acknowledging this strand in the thinking we can see that when Lord Scarman advocated in 1974 the enactment of a Bill of Rights for the United Kingdom it was no accident that he also advocated a new constitutional settlement.[5] Indeed, many would argue – and I believe – that, in the United Kingdom, effective entrenchment of a Bill of Rights is integral with and inseparable from a new constitutional settlement.[6] That consideration, in itself, raises the question as to whether we in the United Kingdom are ready to engage in a great constitutional debate so soon after the abortive arguments about devolution in the 1970s.

The example of New Zealand points to another factor that is relevant to the Bill of Rights argument: the presence in the country of native, indigenous peoples, whose ancestors were there when Europeans arrived to dominate the country. The same phenomenon is found in the United States and in Canada. The history of the treatment by the settlers and their descendants of the native peoples is in no case a history which those who now live in these countries can recall with pride.

In all cases both the history books and the law books record the denial to native peoples of the full rights accorded to those of European stock. In the United States, both for the native peoples and for the imported slaves and their descendants, discrimination was widespread and severe. The Bill of Rights was not written for them.[7] And I suspect that those who practised discrimination against one oppressed minority found it increasingly easy to discriminate against other minorities. The distaste of civilised men for these injustices led, after the Civil War, to attempts to outlaw them by writing into the fundamental law of the country declarations of equality before the law. In the United Kingdom, where slavery was illegal since at least the 18th century,[8] discrimination was practised and legalised against various religious, racial and cultural groups, but equality before the law was the general principle of the Common Law: the many exceptions, usually enacted by a non-democratic Parliament, have gradually been reduced by the legislature and the ordinary courts. The position today is that the law professes the principle of equality; and, although at a social and private level, discrimination and prejudice still exist, the law itself does not in principle deny equality to minority groups in the claiming of their fundamental human rights and immunities. Of course, most of us would acknowledge or even protest about particular instances which illustrate that to be a female or a homosexual or a member of some ethnic or religious minority carries with it certain economic, cultural or other disadvantages, including legal ones, but my point is that the fundamental human rights made available in other Common Law democracies, by the entrenchment of specific and general rights, are not withheld by law in the United Kingdom. Nor is there any political party likely to win power that seeks to deny such rights to such groups. I do not argue that our treatment of minorities is exemplary; merely that our record will stand comparison with that of the USA, where the constitution has always professed freedom and equality.

In New Zealand, the authors of the White Paper,[9] while acknowledging that no government or parliament is likely in the foreseeable future to attempt to sweep away basic rights already recognised by law there, argues that it is much better not to wait for a flood before we build the dam. That may sound sensible; but it cannot mean that we should start building dams in places where there is no foreseeable risk of flood. The conclusion that I would suggest on this point is that, in our society, the absence from our recent history of institutionalised discrimination having its formal origins in the law, and the absence of any recent history of an unholy alliance between the lawmakers and oppressors, make it unnecessary to enact a Bill of Rights to betoken a national repentance for the sins of our forefathers: or to protect us against non-existent threats. The threat of the flood is too remote to warrant the building of a legal dam. The mechanisms of our existing legal and political structures can handle all the foreseeable rainfall.

It would be a bold man who would argue that the Bill of Rights, applied or contemplated in democratic societies whose Common Law is comparable to ours, can succeed in preserving the fundamental rights of the citizens in those countries more effectively than does the ordinary law, as applied in the United Kingdom. No legal mechanisms, entrenched or not, are perfect. No legal system is going to satisfy everybody. No protagonist of the Bill of Rights would argue that it is the gateway to the Promised Land. The practical issues are whether it is necessary, and whether its advantages outweigh its disadvantages – for us. And, in weighing that balance, we should not lose sight of the fact that one of the supposed virtues of a Bill of Rights, the securing – by court decision – of particular rights, can prove illusory. The Supreme Court in Washington can and does overrule its previous decisions. As the composition of the court changes under President Reagan it appears likely that more of the great liberal decisions of the Warren era will be reversed; or as one American critic put it, 'left twisting in the wind'.[10] A Supreme Court can diminish as well as enlarge rights.

In order to provide a degree of flexibility, the Canadian Charter, in common with other modern Bills of Rights, provides that the rights and freedoms it contains are subject to 'such reasonable limits prescribed by law as can be demonstrably justified in a free and democratic society'.[11] But to whom is the legislator to demonstrate such justification? The answer is: the judges. It is the judges who are ultimately to decide what is reasonable and justified in a free and democratic society. Why it should be supposed that elderly lawyers[12] with cautious and backward-looking habits of thought are qualified to overrule the judgments of democratically elected legislators as to what is, in the circumstances of the time, justified, I do not profess to understand. In New Zealand, the protagonists of a Bill of Rights do not seek to conceal that this central provision gives judges the ultimate responsibility for deciding policy questions. And where are their judges to look for guidance in the making of such policy choices? Why, to Canada – to see how Canadian judges, operating a similarly elastic provision, have created answers in the litigations of that country; and also the European Human Rights Court, to the Commonwealth and to the United States. Of course, the opinions of foreign courts are not to be binding. So the judges are left free to pick and choose among the precedents.[13]

There is no escape from the fact that a constitutional provision which gives judges a substantial but ill-defined power to overrule the decisions of Parliament involves a shift of power from elected representatives who are accountable to unelected appointees who are not. To transfer such power to a body of professional specialists is to abdicate a real measure of democratic responsibility. At the moment we are in the odd position that although we have withheld such power from our own judges we have provisionally conceded it to foreign judges by adhering to the European Convention of Human Rights without incorporating it into our domestic law. So, as *The Sunday Times* thalidomide case illustrates, the judges in Strasbourg are empowered by the broad wording of the Convention to strike a different balance between conflicting public interests. In that case, the conflict was between the public interest in freedom of speech and the public interest in the administration of justice. Our judges arrived at one answer.[14] Strasbourg, with a different experience of the press and of the administration of justice, concluded that the law, as declared by the House of Lords, was an interference with freedom of expression, an interference which was not necessary in a democratic society.[15] The case is a telling example of how the interpretation of vaguely worded rights can lead different judges to arrive at novel and different conclusions as to the character and effect of the public interest argument. It is also an example of a field of law in which Parliament itself, a good deal earlier, should have made its own judgment and enacted it.

Some might seek to draw a distinction between a constitutional provision and an entrenched right. I would challenge the validity of any such distinction. The fundamental rights secured and declared in the United States are secured and declared by amendments to the constitution itself. If a document exists and it creates entrenched rights and restrictions it does not matter what you call it. Provided that some mechanism exists for altering the terms of the document, there here is no limit to what can be put into it or taken out of it. It can, as in Ireland, be amended to allow divorce or to deny it; as in America, to prohibit the sale of alcohol[16] or to allow it,[17] to enlarge civil rights or to diminish them, to abolish capital punishment or to permit it. If you can use the mechanism of amendment and command the necessary majorities, you can put into or delete from this fundamental document any selection of rights or restrictions, whatever their character or effect. Of course, amendment is never going to be easy; but the campaigning for and against amendment, whether it is to do with prohibiting the sale of alcohol or with divorce or abortion or contraception or capital punishment or civil rights, demonstrates, if demonstration be needed, that one citizen's right is another citizen's restriction.

A Bill of Rights embodies semi-permanent choices between the conflicting interests of citizens. And to present such choices as if they are the gratuitous enlargement of the human rights of all is to misuse language. Rights are not to be regarded as if they were roses without thorns. Any Bill of Rights which guarantees some rights and denies or conspicuously omits others – for example, economic or cultural rights – is entrenching one set of values at the expense of alternative sets of values.[18] If those whose task it was to select the rights to be protected were to be situated behind a veil of ignorance,[19] so that they did not know how the various alternatives would serve or hinder different interests; if, therefore, they had to choose on the basis of timeless principles acceptable to all right-thinking men; if they were clever enough to choose golden words to express those rights, words so pure and unambiguous that no man, no judge, who had to apply them to real life could possibly fail to ensure that the principles they encapsulated would be applied fairly and equally to all men in all circumstances, then no doubt they could fashion an honest charter of enduring freedoms that would do more than just buttress the interests and values of one class and one generation against the interests and values of their successors.

But how realistic is that hope? A Bill of Rights could serve certain interests and prejudice others. Thus a provision about a right to life would, depending upon how it was phrased by the draftsman and interpreted by the judges, favour one side or the other in the abortion argument.[20] It could hardly avoid doing so. A right of freedom of association is bound to determine or to enable judges to determine, in some degree, and possibly totally, the arguments about the closed shop and collective bargaining.[21] If rights are conferred upon but confined to human persons the results will be entirely different from those which would flow from the conferring of rights upon corporate or legal persons,[22] such as limited companies or trade unions. The essential nature of rights is that they restrict the freedom of those who must respect them. A child's right not to be caned is a restriction upon a teacher's freedom to impose disciplinary sanctions.[23] A worker's right not to join a trade union is a restriction upon the power of his fellow workers to present collectively a monolithic united front to the employer. A right to freedom of speech may be so large, so widely interpreted, that it interferes with the right of accused persons to a fair trial, because it permits the press to publish information which directly or more subtly prejudices the minds of potential jurors or judges.[24] A right to choose freely how one's children are to be educated or one's illnesses are to be treated may confer advantages upon those who can afford to exercise their choice, but leave those who cannot afford to do so with meaningless paper rights. Indeed, the conferring of such rights in relation to education or health care might gravely prejudice the capacity of the community as a whole to allocate and distribute limited educational and health care resources in such a way as to benefit those in need or those who can benefit, rather than those who can pay. The point of offering such examples is not to indicate a preference for or against abortion, the closed shop, private medicine or public schools. The point is that these matters, and countless others, involve political choices. And their character does not alter because they are cast in the noble language of fundamental human rights.

Bear in mind that one of the principal arguments for conferring certain rights in an entrenched charter is that they should not be able to be disturbed by a temporary political majority which in a parliamentary democracy commands the legislature and executive for five or ten years.

Of course that argument has some force; particularly for those who cannot win such a majority, because it opens up for them a route for obtaining and preserving rights which the majority want to modify or remove. But it also means that if a particular coalition of interest groups can at the moment of enactment of the charter win a sufficient majority to ensure that their interest is secured and entrenched in the form of a charter right, then later parliamentary majorities cannot adjust that and related rights in accordance with the wishes of the majority. Charters of entrenched rights provide a favourable environment for the single-issue fanatics, such as the American Prohibitionists of the 1920s. The 18th Amendment introducing Prohibition has been described as the crowning achievement of a movement which had become the 'rallying-point of those who wished to save the Republic from the corrupting effects of alcohol, the saloon, machine politics, jazz and the movies, from all the sins which robbed the nation of its purity'.[25]

Even if, when the charter is enacted, there is no consensus to frame a particular interest as an explicit right, it may well be possible to smuggle it in, in a vague and delphic form of words, leaving alive the hope that by interpretation judges will ultimately make explicit that which the charter left obscure. So the power lies with the judges. The real alternatives are not, on the one hand, some timeless noble document which eloquently distils and expresses the best essence of civilised experience and, on the other, an elective dictatorship abusing its temporary stewardship by trampling on the rights of minorities.

What are the alternatives? On the one hand, we can make political choices and buttress them against change – whether they are spelled out explicitly or left to be teased out of the wording by the judges. On the other, we can leave such choices to be made and remade, by elected representatives who must answer to the electorate for their decisions. As time passes, the alternatives can surely become rule by the words of yesterday's charter majority as filtered through the minds of today's judges versus rule by today's elected representatives.

To leave profound policy issues to judges in this way is to avoid a principled and fully informed consideration by society itself of the problem of where in a civilised and free society the lines fall to be drawn and the balances struck.[26] If the judges are required to put flesh on the bare bones of vaguely worded rights, where are they to draw their inspiration from? They may choose to look at the United States, which has had to address such questions; but they will find some funny answers. The Supreme Court has had to consider, for example, what limits, if any, fall to be placed on the freedom of speech guaranteed in the First Amendment and how that freedom can be squared with the Sixth Amendment guarantee of a fair trial by an impartial jury or the Fourteenth Amendment guarantee of due process. In the result, the media can carry almost unrestricted information about the life and circumstances of a person who is to face trial on criminal charges even though potential jurors may read that information and be prejudiced by it. So it may take weeks to select a jury and it may have to consist of people who read no newspapers and watch no television. We in Britain would treat such publication as being in contempt of court, because we think that the need to ensure a fair trial overrides the need to sell newspapers. Why should the judgment of Parliament on such a matter be abdicated to judges, even if, as our history suggests, the judges would, in that particular case, probably make a good job of it?[27]

In the United States, the judges have hardly been uniformly and conspicuously successful, by comparison with the United Kingdom, in securing and extending fundamental human rights and freedoms. What are held by some as the glittering achievements of the United States Supreme Court in asserting civil liberties or fundamental rights fail to be seen in their context. The advances in human rights achieved in the Supreme Court can be assessed only against the background. Occasionally, that background is so oppressive, so prejudiced and so cruel that one is left wondering how a society conceived with such nobility of rhetoric and purpose could have created such oppression, inequality and prejudice. That is an historical matter. But a lawyer who tried to form a picture of American society by reading nothing but the reports of cases in the Supreme Court would end up with a depressing view of that society.[28]

In studying even recent liberal decisions of the Supreme Court one tends to break off from applauding the answers in sheer dismay that it was still necessary to ask the questions.[29] Sometimes even the answers cause equal dismay. The Supreme Court has, for the past three decades or so, advanced the cause of human rights against the opposition not just of those opposed to such rights but also of those who believed that the unelected judges have no warrant in the constitution for such judicial activism. But even on the human rights front if we go back beyond the 1950s we find a history of the court's reluctance to use the same Bill of Rights for the same purpose. As Justice Thurgood Marshall, the first black to sit on the bench of the Supreme Court, said in a case in 1978: 'During most of the past 200 years, the constitution as interpreted by this court did not prohibit the most ingenious and pervasive forms of discrimination against the Negro.'[30]

I do not seek to deny that recently much has been achieved both in civil rights and elsewhere. But even the broad, unqualified statements of rights which the Supreme Court Justices have had to apply did not prevent them, until recently, from taking a narrow, legalistic, laissez-faire perspective on freedom so as to strike down as unconstitutional legislation designed to stop the exploitation of workers, women, children or immigrants.[31] They legalised slavery,[32] and when it was abolished, they legalised racial segregation.[33] They repeatedly held that women were not entitled to equality with men.[34] They approved the unconstitutional removal by the Executive of the constitutional rights of Americans of Japanese origin after the bombing of Pearl Harbour.[35]

In truth, statements of fundamental rights can seldom be enacted with precision. They are full of notions like 'due process' or 'respect for family life' or 'freedom to manifest one's religion'. And the rights are then qualified by equally elastic concepts, like 'reasonable', or 'necessary in a free society' or 'national security'. When rights are created in vague and imprecise terms, their content to be discovered by judges whose choices are not determined by familiar and well understood rules of law, no one really knows, till the courts have decided, what his rights are.

So, unless it can be shown that it is, on balance, necessary to enact a Bill of Rights to enable our citizens to achieve rights not available through the processes of democracy, unless it can be shown that we can agree on the content, and the precise expression, of particular rights, we should be slow to confer upon our judges an unreviewable power to evolve a miscellany of actual rights and restraints whose real content we cannot sensibly predict.

However inconvenient and untidy it is for our judges to have to stand aside and observe European judges, whether in Luxembourg[36] or in Strasbourg, decide human rights and discrimination questions on the basis of materials not available to the domestic courts, that is not an argument for creating the great cloud of uncertainty that a domestic Bill of Rights would bring.

CHAPTER SIX

LIONS UNDER THE THRONE

•

'The life of the law has not been logic,' said Oliver Wendell Holmes, 'it has been experience.' That experience included, he said, 'the prejudices which judges share with their fellow men'.[1] No one could dispute that judges are likely to share the prejudices of their fellow men; though it is more common for the details of such prejudices to be disclosed by historians than by contemporary studies of serving judges.[2] And prejudices, though they may fall into patterns, are selective. The prejudices of elderly, white, affluent males are bound to be different from the prejudices of young, black, impoverished females. So there is limited reassurance to be found in the fact that some others in a particular society share the same prejudices as some judges, or that some of a judge's prejudices are shared by some of his fellow citizens. But does it matter if a judge has a few prejudices, provided he keeps quiet about them? Well, obviously it does not matter if the prejudices are irrelevant to the dispute which is being judicially considered. A particular judge might harbour a prejudice about Rastafarians or second-hand car salesmen, but it would hardly affect his or her capacity to decide a patent case between two public companies.

The other side of the coin is that it doesn't matter provided that care is taken to ensure that, as far as possible, issues on which judges are likely to have significant and relevant prejudices are not remitted to them for decision. Judges will no doubt do their human and professional best to eliminate from their reasoning and decision-making the distorting effects of prejudice. But even at that, it must be conceded that the influence of prejudice must not only be avoided: it must be *seen* to be avoided. So it is better, if possible, not to require judges to decide cases – particularly cases which make new law – in which their prejudices might be thought capable of influencing their thinking. In this regard, too, there are lessons that may be learned from the United States experience.

In that country, because there is a written constitution, all issues can be translated into justifiable legal disputes, and most are. No one there assumes that judges are totally free from prejudice. The necessary result is that the appointment of federal judges, and especially of justices of the Supreme Court, has become a highly sensitive political issue. The history of the appointment of justices to the United States Supreme Court illustrates how the political and social characteristics of the appointees are important – so important that almost every proposed appointment comes to be scrutinised with particular care.

Pressure groups with interests in such matters as abortion, civil rights, religion or pornography, study the background of possible appointees with a view to alerting the Senate to those strands in the candidate's make-up and history which are thought likely to play a part in shaping his judgment in such matters when he comes to cast his vote. They are not wrong to do so. The votes of the appointed justices are likely to lay down the law in these fields, in all of which the Constitution is deemed to have a determining influence. And each single vote can be vital. Numerous cases of great importance have been decided by a single vote.[3]

Examples include the *Miranda* case,[4] which I described earlier, in which vitally important fundamental rights were secured for persons questioned while in police custody on suspicion of having committed a crime. In *Mapp* v. *Ohio*,[5] which created the modern exclusionary rule – under which evidence obtained by searches and seizures in violation of the Constitution is inadmissible in a criminal trial – four out of the nine justices disagreed with the other five who constituted the majority. In the recent *Bakke* case, a white student challenged the right of the University of California to operate an admissions programme which allocated some of the places exclusively to members of ethnic minorities, and thus raised the legal and constitutional issue as to whether or not positive discrimination in favour of such minorities was permitted by a law which prescribed equality. He found four justices in favour of the view that it did; and four against. The ninth in effect said, 'maybe in some cases, but not in this', and Mr Bakke succeeded.[6] But the underlying issue as to the meaning of equality was not finally resolved.

The background history of one of the most important American cases of modern times, *Brown* v. *The Board of Education*,[7] is an equally striking example of the importance of the personnel; for only the sudden death of Chief Justice Vinson and his replacement by the bold and liberal-minded Earl Warren enabled the court to avoid a split-decision on the question of whether or not the Constitution prohibited the provision by a state of separate schools for blacks.[8]

The political composition and character of the Supreme Court has always been important, but its importance became dramatically realised in the 1930s after the court had, in a succession of cases, struck down as unconstitutional a number of the New Deal measures introduced by President Roosevelt. These rulings led Roosevelt to try to pack the court with favourable judges. In the event he did not have to do so, because the court changed its mind – or at least one of its nine members did, and the court began to hold the New Deal legislation constitutional and valid.[9] But no President since Roosevelt has failed to appreciate the importance of trying to have the right men on the court. Richard Nixon, in campaigning for office, promised that his appointees to the Supreme Court would be 'different'. In 1980 the Republican Party pledged itself to 'work for the appointment at all levels of judges who respected traditional values and the sanctity of innocent human life;' in other words, judges who opposed abortion, but, inferentially, did not oppose capital punishment.[10] President Carter warned the National Association for the Advancement of Coloured Peoples that their civil rights could be adversely affected if the Republicans got another three or four appointments to the Supreme Court.[11] At the present time, with several justices nearing 80 years of age, there is a reasonable prospect that before he leaves office President Reagan will have nominated a substantial number of justices, as many of his predecessors, including Presidents Roosevelt and Nixon, did.[12] A 'Reagan' court could then be determining constitutional issues for perhaps 10 or 15 years and would be likely to adopt a different approach to such questions as abortion, presidential power, police powers and even civil rights from the court once presided over by Chief Justice Warren.

It would be naive to suppose that in selecting persons to nominate, a President would pay no attention whatsoever to the political and social attitudes which such persons might bring to bear when determining the types of question which they would encounter while holding office as justices of the Supreme Court.[13] One recent analysis of President Reagan's appointees to the federal bench discloses that 98 per cent of his appointees were white, 98 per cent were Republicans and 92 per cent were male. The Senate, which has a right of veto, also questions nominees at great length, with a view to determining how they are likely to turn out as arbiters of great public issues. That is inevitable in a country where the Supreme Court – by interpreting a Bill of Rights – often determines such issues. It appears equally inevitable that the enactment here – particularly if it could be successfully entrenched – of a Bill of Rights in vague and imprecise terms of the kind that characterise the wording of such Bills of Rights, would force those who in this country appoint judges to have regard to the philosophical, political and social outlook of those who would have the ultimate responsibility of deciding the political and social questions certain to rise under such a Bill.

It must be remembered that it is not just in the United States that the highest court decides important cases by the narrowest of majorities, sometimes reversing the decisions by law courts in doing so. I have already given some British examples but there are many more known to practising lawyers.

We in this country have slowly moved away from the appointment of judges on a political basis[14] and have become very sensitive to the danger of requiring judges to decide purely political questions or, indeed, legal questions that have enduring political importance. That sensitivity is one of the features that have characterised the debate about the role of the law in industrial relations. But it applies more widely than that; it may apply to such questions as immigration, criminal-law enforcement, education, homelessness, police powers or many other such issues in which the courts, even when applying the ordinary law, tend increasingly to become involved.[15] There is, I believe, no escape from the fact that if judges are required, in addition, to interpret and apply a vaguely worded Charter of Human Rights, they will inevitably be drawn into the political arena in a way that neither they nor many others would welcome.

It is, I think, impossible to measure the degree to which the known or supposed political or philosophical leanings of candidates for judicial office could come to influence their selection and promotion; but I believe the influence would be real. Under the present systems for the appointment of judges both north and south of the border, the persons who select, appoint and promote judges are the politicians who currently hold certain of the great offices of state.[16] If, as a result of enacting a Bill of Rights, issues which are now decided in Parliament come to be litigated in the courts and decided by judges, then the cast of mind of the members of the higher judiciary will inevitably become a matter of profound political interest. The question whether the candidate is of a liberal or a conservative disposition is likely to be relevant. Is he a strict constructionist or an imaginative interventionist? As it happens almost all current members of the higher tiers of the judiciary, both in England and Scotland, were selected for promotion by Conservative prime ministers. They include, with only one exception,[17] all the Lords of Appeal, the Lord Chief Justice, the Master of the Rolls, the President of the Family Division, the Lord President of the Court of Session and the Lord Justice Clerk.[18] No one, so far as I am aware, has found this very remarkable or disturbing; nor should it be. But if the higher courts had to resolve the issues that a Bill of Rights would bring before judges, then such considerations must become relevant, just as in the USA.

William Paley, writing in 1785, said: 'The first maxim of a free state is that the laws be made by one set of men, and administered by another.' It is that separation of powers which is put at risk if judges are empowered to make and unmake laws, by interpreting a Bill of Rights which requires them to make policy choices.

If, as I have argued, we do not need to enact a Bill of Rights in order to secure the kinds of human rights that we want our citizens to enjoy, because such rights are already tolerably well secured or at least achievable by means of existing mechanisms; if we have, as we do, methanisms, both in the European Convention and even through the Court of the European Communities in Luxembourg, for keeping a watch, albeit an imperfect one, upon human rights in an international context, then we do not need to put at risk the political impartiality of judges in order to seek to secure an uncertain gain of nebulous character.

If I am right in suggesting that the present role of judges deserves reasessment, at least in certain fields, and that the temptation greatly to expand their role and jurisdiction is to be resisted, what should judges be doing that is not already being satisfactorily done? Their real role is to adjudicate in particular disputes by applying the law competently and impartially; ideally, that involves that disputes be resolved as swiftly, as cheaply and as justly as is humanly possible. Of course these objectives are not easily reconcilable. The cheapest and swiftest way to settle a dispute is to toss a coin, but justice according to law is lost. But if the search for a perfect justice according to law becomes unduly protracted and expensive, confidence in the judicial system is diminished; and too many who feel aggrieved conclude that the search is not worth undertaking or continuing. No one can be satisfied with the administration of justice as it is today. The delays, costs and complexities are notorious. No doubt they have been worse at other times and are worse in other countries, but that is no comfort to the potential litigant. And the problems do not yield readily to administrative solutions, such as providing more judges or building more courts or spending more on legal aid, however necessary or desirable such measures appear to be. The problems are radical. They derive from our tradition of an adversarial system, in which the parties' legal advisers are allowed a leisurely timetable to prepare each case for a set-piece confrontation, to be conducted orally before a non-intervening umpire who has only limited powers to shape or restrict the range of the inquiry, and who is fettered by rules of evidence, such as the rules against hearsay evidence or the right to silence, rules which evolved in circumstances that no longer obtain.

It would be a short step from that analysis to conclude that by turning our judges into inquisitors we can throw off a great burden of inherited procedure and create a swift and inexpensive system under which the judge is liberated so as to achieve instant justice. But it would, I fear, be a serious error to suppose that such a dramatic departure from the systems we have evolved in the United Kingdom would readily and easily give us, or enable judges to give litigants, justice that would be swift, certain, cheap and sure. In the first place, it does not appear that inquisitorial systems elsewhere prove to be quicker, cheaper or better. In the second, our judges have no substantial training or experience that enables them to be inquisitors or conciliators. Their traditional skill as judges is in the analysis and assessment of competing contentions which have been carefully fashioned by the lawyers acting for the conflicting interests. They employ that skill not to decide what is good, but what is better; not what is true, but what is more probable; not what is, but what is proved to be.[19]

What, I believe, is needed to engage the judge's experience of making such judgments at a much earlier stage in litigation, particularly civil litigation, so that he plays a substantial part in defining and articulating the issues which are justiciable and which have to be resolved. Our present procedures allow too much time for each party to set out his stall before the judge is brought in to judge the competition. Looking at each case individually, there is obviously merit in allowing litigants to investigate, manoeuvre, negotiate, compromise and prepare so that eventually, if necessary, they can each lay before the court a finely honed presentation of the most favourable evidence and argument. But, when one stands back and looks at litigation from a wider perspective, one sees a system in which the final outcome of too many cases is delayed for years, a system in which the protracted procedures lead to unconscionable delay and expense. Litigation is seldom just a private affair in which the litigants alone are affected. Even if it were, most litigants want their cases decided quickly so that they can get on with the rest of their lives. The uncertainties and worries of a long drawn-out litigation can seriously disturb the happiness and well-being of the litigant, who finds the processes of the law Kafkaesque. But many cases directly or indirectly affect others not themselves parties to the litigation. The most obvious examples are the children affected by long drawn-out family disputes, or the families of those whose financial future depends upon the fate of a claim for damages for personal injury. We cannot rest content with a system in which the ordinary litigant finds himself joining a queue which shuffles fitfully towards an uncertain destination.

I have quite deliberately refrained in these lectures from describing the features of Scottish law and the procedure which make it distinctive, if only because their interest to most listeners would be, at best, wholly academic. But allow me to summarise briefly one Scottish criminal rule of outstanding value, which might be copied by others, and the principle of which could be extended even in Scotland. We call it the 110-day rule. In essence it provides that no person can be detained in prison for more than 110 days before being brought to trial, though some discretion is allowed for exceptional circumstances.[20] The obvious benefit of the rule is that it reduces to a minimum the scandal of untried prisoners being jailed awaiting trials which not infrequently result in their acquittal. The most striking effect of the rule is that those who are responsible for investigating and prosecuting serious crime are obliged to prepare and present their cases with the utmost urgency, so that such cases are tried while the evidence is fresh. It concentrates the prosecutor's mind wonderfully, because if it is not observed, the accused goes free. But the most remarkable feature of the rule is that it works.[21] If it can work in Scotland, it can work elsewhere. If we can, as we must, bring cases of murder, rape or serious drug-trafficking to trial within four months of arrest, the same can be done elsewhere in the United Kingdom. Not only that; if we can bring murder cases to trial within four months, we demonstrate, even to ourselves, that the complexities of procedure, the rules of evidence and the requirements of fairness do not constitute insuperable obstacles to the speedy resolution of serious litigation. We demonstrate that undue delay is not a necessary ingredient in the processes of justice. If murder trials involving difficult questions of fact and law can be brought to a conclusion within months, why should it take years to decide cases of medical negligence, industrial accident, custody of children or breach of contract? What the success of the 110-day rule illustrates is that if you design a peremptory time-limit into litigation procedure, lawyers will adapt their preparations accordingly. Indeed this is done in other types of case, including administrative review cases. It may be argued that there is a serious shortage of judicial time. There is. But in fact the judges and the courts do hear all the contested cases eventually, so the factor of judicial time is a constant in the equation. What we have is a classic backlog problem. The challenge is to find ways of bringing cases to fruition earlier rather than later. It would be impossible to move overnight to a system which brought most cases to trial within a short timescale. But if we will the end, we must will the means. In criminal cases, for example, consideration could be given to the Continental device of an amnesty, designed to clear the system of the backlog of those cases in which society's interest in securing conviction is sufficiently slight to be traded off against promoting society's interest in accelerating trials in more important cases.

At first blush, the idea of deliberately announcing that some offenders are not to be prosecuted might startle those who believe that the rule of law itself requires that offenders should be tried and punished. But, as it is, we catch and convict only a fraction of offenders.[22] Even when they are caught, significant numbers are not brought to trial, for a variety of reasons including administrative ones. There have even been examples of those fields of law-breaking in which it has been deliberately decided not to prosecute, for reasons of public policy.[23] So, to announce an amnesty would only be to extend and formalise existing practices and make them more uniform. The problems of choosing which offences or offenders should fall under an amnesty are formidable; but we cannot, without trying, conclude that they are insuperable. Lawyers and penologists are familiar with the broad distinction between crimes which are wicked in themselves and conduct which is punishable only because it is prohibited by statutory regulation. So we have a starting-point. Even if on such a basis we amnestied only the comparatively minor offences, we could save much police and court time and, and could consider redistributing slightly more serious cases to the lower courts whose docket had been relieved by the amnesty.

Of course the backlog of civil cases could hardly be disposed of in this way; no one has or should have the right to kill off the proceedings in civil cases just because their presence in the rolls is blocking the disposal of other, more recent cases. So it is not easy to devise a procedural remedy to achieve instantly what generations of judges, lawyers and administrators have failed to achieve in their assiduous attempts to speed up litigation without diluting the quality of justice. But I believe that a principal reason for our failures hitherto has been our reluctance to depart from the central notion that the way to dispose of the cases which cannot be compromised is to have a set-piece battle, in public, before a judge who comes as a stranger to the case. In such proceedings the contestants battle for the judge's decision in a highly formalised ritual in which the judge's role is essentially passive, a ritual in which he is the one-man jury.

This form of trial is excellent for certain types of difficult case. But it does not really offer much scope for one of the skills that any competent judge must have acquired in the course of his career as an advocate: the skill to home in on the essentials of a case. A great many cases raise only a few sharply contested issues, whether of fact or of law. The advocate's task is to cut through all the detail and identify the several points on which the case is likely to turn. It is that same skill that the judge brings to bear when he comes to decide a case or to present it for decision to a jury. What our procedures neglect to do is to provide an early and informal opportunity for the impartial judge to come into the case to assist the parties to identify those few questions which cannot be resolved except by means of the formalised forensic battle. He is given no responsibility or even opportunity to apply firm pressure on the parties at an early stage to clear the ground so as to move to a speedy resolution of the matters that have to go to formal trial. I emphasise the question of informality because our formal procedures tend to keep litigants at arm's length, and because this very formality causes both delay and expense.

One of the most striking features of our systems of litigation, particularly but not exclusively in civil cases, is how many cases are settled on the very eve of the formal court hearing. The real reason for that is that the prospect of having to demonstrate the merits of the case before an impartial court compels litigants and their lawyers to make a realistic assessment of their prospects; they know they have to take the cards from their chest and lay them face up on the table. The long, expensive period of bluff and bluster has come to an end. What I suggest we have to do is to devise a method whereby the judge comes in as early as possible to compel litigants to face up to their respective weaknesses and strengths. A judge would not lose his impartiality by giving his provisional views as to the true shape of the issues in a dispute; and if it were felt that the informal processes had put his objectivity at risk, the issues which still remained to be ventilated and decided could be put before a different judge. I would not advocate turning judges into inquisitors who would conduct investigations, or even into conciliators who would try to bang heads together. I merely suggest that we should be more ready to see the courts, notably in civil cases, as being there to provide a social service, the service of helping the citizens as informally as possible either to resolve their disputes or to limit the questions at issue to those which really need the Rolls-Royce treatment of a full-blown trial. We have something to learn from the informal procedures of arbitrations and tribunals. We must slaughter a few sacred cows inherited from our history, and refashion our very language, our forms, our rituals, our rules of evidence, our procedures in order to provide more swiftly and more cheaply a justice that loses nothing by being seen as a social service.

I began these lectures by talking about one form of temptation. As I end them I am conscious of others. In particular, I am tempted to bow out with grandiloquent assertions about the majesty and nobility of the law, to persuade you how lucky you all are that the rule of law, the administration of justice and the traditions of a powerful independent judiciary are still safe in the dependable hands of Her Majesty's judges. Instead, I find myself talking about the nuts-and-bolts of court procedure. I hope I need make no apology for that. The value of a system of justice is not to be measured by the rhetoric of its apologists or the garments it wears, but in the speed, the price and the availability of the remedies it affords for the redress of grievance. And if we are tempted to forget that, and to suppose that judges would be better employed pursuing an altogether loftier and more visible role in those political and constitutional fields now exclusively occupied by others, we will, like F. E. Smith, have allowed our brains to go to our heads.[24]

No doubt we have much to learn from others. Without doubt the exercise by the Supreme Court of its great *imperium* has been, on the whole, a force for good in the United States. That court was, it has been said, the world's first human rights tribunal.[25] It is still, by far, the only one whose jurisprudence and history are rich enough to yield real lessons for other common law countries. But the legal buttressing of our liberties has been achieved without placing legal lions under the throne.[25] If, for less than compelling reasons, we now seek to put them there, we will be taking a giant step away from a tradition that has served us well. And we will have shut our eyes to the essential lesson of democracy, that 'the great fundamental decisions that determine the course of society must ultimately be made by society itself'.

I cannot do better than to end with the words of the American judge, Learned Hand: 'I often wonder whether we do not rest our hopes too much upon constitutions, upon laws and upon courts. These are false hopes; believe me, these are false hopes. Liberty lies in the hearts of men and women; when it dies there no constitution, no law, no court can save it; no constitution, no law, no court can even do much to help it. While it lies there it needs no constitution, no law, no court to save it.'[26]

DISCUSSION

In accordance with the tradition of the Reith lectures the BBC invited the author to discuss his themes with distinguished critics. The Lord Chancellor, Lord Hailsham of St. Marylebone has repeatedly warned of the potential threat to liberty inherent in some theories of the sovereignty of parliament. Lord Scarman has long been the most eloquent judicial advocate for enacting a new bill of rights. Professor Ian Kennedy, a former Reith lecturer, chaired the discussion.

CHAIRMAN: Lord McCluskey, the title of your lectures was *Law, Justice and Democracy*. The dominant theme for me, was the role of the judge in a democracy such as ours. Inevitably, you were drawn to consider the question of a Bill of Rights. Whether we needed one. What would it mean for us? Perhaps you could start by briefly outlining your views.

MCCLUSKEY: Well I think my primary purpose was to look to see where judges come from, if I can put it like that. I am not interested in the lectures in looking at the social or the educational, or if you like, the political background of judges. I was interested in discovering where a judge is promoted from. And my answer was, and is, that judges are essentially lawyers who act for clients. They are successful at that; and after a quarter of a century, concerning themselves with what the law is, and how it can be fashioned in order to assist their clients, they then arrive on the Bench with that kind of expertise, knowing what the law is. Then they have to apply the law to what they determine are the facts in a particular case. Now I think that is an excellent training for the kind of judges that we use for the ordinary type of case. But there's a vast difference between an expertise in knowing what the law is, and an expertise in deciding what the law *should* be; and I think therefore that once you start to give judges a wider charter, whether it be of rights or (in any shape or form) give them a breadth that law and their practice doesn't give them, then they become legislators more and more and more.

SCARMAN: I basically agree with Lord McCluskey, of course, that judges are concerned with legal principles and not policy choices. I fail to understand how it can be said that applying, for instance, a Bill of Rights, if one was enacted, involves the judge in policy choices and not in legal principles. Of course judges are concerned with the law as it is. Of course they are concerned with applying that law to particular circumstances.

Of course they have to be lawyers, which means under our system, they have to be trained in the adversarial system. Just as well, because if they are going to become judges, they have got to operate it, and they've got to know how it works, its weaknesses and its strengths.

HAILSHAM: Well of course it's true that in the Common law world, our judges are made out of successful advocates. In fact, that is the exception in the civilised world, and not the rule. In all the European countries, and the civil law countries, the judicial career is separate from the forensic career. Personally I prefer our system; but where I think I differ slightly from Lord McCluskey, is this. Of course judges are not legislators. And where a statute enacted by Parliament lays down what the law is, the judges – well they have got to conform. But I suppose a very sizeable proportion of our most important legal rules are customary law, and what a judge has got to do is not only to come to a conclusion which is in conformity with his own conscience, but he's got to build it into a coherent mass, with the existing body of legal doctrine. And I do think therefore the law will never be the same after the judge has decided his case, as it was before.

KENNEDY: But aren't we a bit ahead of ourselves in worrying about who's going to interpret the Bill of Rights? Surely the first question is whether we need a Bill of Rights.

LORD MCCLUSKEY: Well, yes that is an important question, but I don't know that it matters which one is the first question because they both have to be answered before you ultimately take the decision. But I still think you have got to ask how it's going to work. There's much to be proud of in the history of British judges. What I am saying is this, that if you give them a vague charter, then you really turn them into instant legislators.

SCARMAN: I don't accept the assumption that a Bill of Rights is a vague charter. I don't accept that a Bill of Rights is any vaguer than Common Law principles, which are our customary law. When you ask the question 'Can a judge successfully interpret and apply the will of Parliament as expressed in the Bill of Rights, or is it too vague for him?' My reply is: recall what judges have been doing with the Common Law. The Common Law is a set of flexible principles which as the Lord Chancellor has pointed out, develop over the years, responding to social and economic circumstances; and there is really nothing more difficult than dealing with customary law, keeping it within the bounds of precedent, and allowing it to develop.

HAILSHAM: I think if you'd asked me twenty years ago whether I believed in a Bill of Rights, I would have said that the American amendments to their constitution and so on, belonged to an earlier stage of development. The struggle for freedom when they tried to formulate in a series of simple propositions, what they meant by their rights. Now I don't think that now anymore for this reason. Rightly or wrongly, we have got a Bill of Rights. We have signed the European Convention on Human Rights, which happens to follow that type of formula, and what we have done is to put ourselves in the hands of judges at Strasbourg, instead of putting ourselves in the hands of judges in Westminster or Edinburgh. Now personally, I mean no disrespect to the judges of Strasbourg, I think the judges at Edinburgh or Westminster or Belfast have a better feel for the way in which those rights to which we are committed in international law, ought to be applied in the English, Scottish or Northern Irish context, than the chaps at Strasbourg, and therefore I have always given my vote, in recent years, for something on the lines of Lord Scarman's legislative proposals, which he's put forward more than once.

SCARMAN: And I might just add this, I strongly agree with what the Lord Chancellor has just said. Now I'd like to put this to you Lord McCluskey, two things about a Bill of Rights, founded as the present proposal is, on our international obligation under the European Convention of Human Rights, such a Bill of Rights actually covers Common Law concepts. The first Bill of Rights was introduced by the Americans as amendments to their constitution. They were in fact English lawyers, brought up in the Middle Temple and other Inns, making sure that for the protection of individuals and the States, the individual States, the English Common Law, with the powers of the Monarch removed, should become the charter for basic human rights. Now, the American Bill of Rights is a very Common Law Document. Strangely enough the European Convention of Human Rights, borrows an enormous amount from the American Bill of Rights. Indeed, we know as a matter of history that much of its drafting was done by two very distinguished English lawyers, one of whom was later a Lord Chancellor. Therefore, it really is a chimera to think that the Bill of Rights is something so vague, and so uncertain that it will mystify British Judges. It is no more uncertain than the Common Law, and indeed I would say it was very much more precise, and it has this advantage. A Bill of Rights, for it to be considered by our judges, would have to be an Act of Parliament. That means Parliament has made the policy choice. Those policy choices are contained in the articles of a Bill of Rights. The judge's job is to interpret and apply the words of an Act of Parliament which Parliament has thought it good policy to introduce into the law. I do believe we are on a completely bad point in suggesting that the Bill of Rights is something too vague and too uncertain for British judges, trained as they are, to apply and enforce.

MCCLUSKEY: And I must have expressed myself rather badly to suggest to you that the Bill of Rights would mystify, I should say, mystify and puzzle British judges. I don't think that's what I'm saying. What I am saying is it liberates them from the law, to decide whatever they feel is proper in the particular case. And you say Parliament by enacting the Bill, or putting the European Convention into British law, makes the choices. Not at all. By opting for such vague notions, as privacy or against cruel and inhuman punishment, or whatever it may be, it leaves the actual choice to somebody else. I mean do you imagine that in 1953, when the European Convention was drafted, that people actually addressed their minds as to whether birching was allowed in the Isle of Man, or whether Scottish schoolteachers could use the strap? But these decisions had then to be made by the 21 judges in Strasbourg.

SCARMAN: Lord McCluskey, could I ask you this question before we leave a Bill of Rights. With respect, I've found lacking really in your lectures an indication of the possible *value* of a Charter of Human Rights in English law. Let me in one sentence, put to you what I suggest is the value. If you have a Bill of Rights, that's a charter of the human rights and freedoms to be protected by law, i.e. protected in our courts (to pick up the point of the Lord Chancellor). The advantage will be this. You will have an independent judiciary because the judges act through decisions in court, applying and enforcing where necessary, not policies but legal principles of conduct upon the executive arm of Government. Now, the traditional role of British judges has been to keep the executive within the law. That's a very limited role. Never touches the executive policy. The Bill of Rights strengthens that function, that traditional function, of our independent judiciary.

MCCLUSKEY: Yes, well I think if you go to the history, and the modern history, of the American Supreme Court, you get the answer to that, which is that policy choices, political choices, are dressed up as the application of legal principle, and that's what I'm afraid of.

SCARMAN: Yes, well I don't want to get into a discussion at the moment about the American example, which I agree, looms large in your lectures. But I suggest that the American experience, though valuable and exciting, is not always relevant.

KENNEDY: I must say that was a point that I took also: that I am sure it's very difficult to extrapolate from the United States and its circumstances to ours, and I am not sure that always using examples of difficulties the

United States Supreme Court has encountered is a good argument. Can I pick up what Lord Scarman was saying a moment ago about judicial checking, if you will, or examining executive action, because one area of judicial activism, or a development in judicial behaviour, which you appear to approve of, Lord McCluskey, is what we call judicial review or the review by the courts of administrative action. Lord Hailsham, do you view with approval the development we've seen over the last 30 years of the judiciary looking very closely at what the Executive may have done?

HAILSHAM: Yes I do, although of course, it's not a course in the least limited to the Executive. It covers subordinate bodies and the Executive is a subordinate body, under our Constitution, of all sorts. I think the original way in which this developed, until about 1977, was much too rigid and much too formalised. But it still remains, however much it may have expanded, it is an attack upon the processes by which decisions are arrived at, and not an attack upon the substantive law. If Parliament says in one case 'This shall be the law,' the judges have got to take it. But if, on the other hand, it watches a Minister and says 'Look you've taken into account irrelevant matters, or failed to take into account relevant matters, or if you've gone outside the powers which Parliament gave' or if it says that to a county council, or to any subordinate body, a rent tribunal or whatever, I think this is on the whole benevolent. It can go too far, of course it can go too far; but I think on the whole it's a benevolent jurisdiction.

KENNEDY: Lord McCluskey, you seem to approve, if I may say so, of this development if only because it's the judiciary checking administrators rather than Parliament as the Lord Chancellor has put it. But you also hint, do you not, that this may be the replay, or the refighting of an old constitutional battle where the judges are beginning to take on Parliament? If that is the case, presumably you wouldn't therafter approve of it?

MCCLUSKEY: Well let me first of all just pick up Lord Hailsham's point, and I'll use the term judicial review, although technically there's a better term, but that's the most understood one. Now when the judges look to ensure that the administrators of whatever kind, stay within the limits that Parliament or the law has imposed upon them, I totally and utterly approve of that, and that's the proper function of the courts. When the judges step beyond that, if they do, and some of the supporters of judicial review say they do, and applaud them for it, when they do that, and begin then to defy Parliament, to rebel against Parliament as one of the supporters put it, then I don't approve of that, and I don't imagine that either Lord Hailsham or Lord Scarman would approve of that, unless Parliament had said, by enacting a Bill of Rights, 'You have the power to review our legislation in that way.' So I draw the distinction between narrow judicial review of administrative action to ensure that people stay within the powers conferred upon them and the broader, substantive due process type of review which looks behind the forms of action and looks at the rationale, and remakes the policy choices that should be left to others.

SCARMAN: I agree with Lord McCluskey, under our law judges certainly may not defy, cannot defy, the legislative will of Parliament, and we have a constitution even though it isn't a written one, but parts of it are in writing, and one part of that constitution which is in writing, is that the judges will obey the legislative will of Parliament. This is vital. If I thought there was anything in the proposal for a Bill of Rights in this country, which empowered judges to defy Parliament, I should say simply: that is unconstitutional. The great difference, of course, between America and Great Britain is they have a written constitution. The judiciary have a specific constitutional role, and that they carry out. That constitutional role is not possessed by our judges and there's nothing in a Bill of Rights which requires judges to exercise that sort of constitutional power in regard to legislation. The truth of the matter is that judges are far more likely to trouble Parliament by a development of Common Law principle which doesn't originate from Parliament, than they are to trouble Parliament by interpreting broadly, and in accordance with a legislative purpose, a statute called a Bill of Rights.

HAILSHAM: I did say a moment ago, that I thought there was a danger that the thing might go too far. I think I agree with McCluskey, it can go too far, but I think in the last ten years, particularly in the judicial capacity of the House of Lords, Lord Diplock, the late Lord Diplock in particular, has really laid out the guidelines definitively. The other thing I wanted to say in this field of judicial review, is that the difference between us and other countries (almost every other country) is not that we have no written constitution; a great deal of our constitutional law is in writing. But in other countries, constitutional law is a different kind of law, a different body of law. It has to be decided by special courts. It can be changed only by special means, plebiscites or whatever, and in our law, constitutional law is partly convention, and partly because of the ordinary body of English law, decided by the same courts (I am sorry, English, I should have said British) but decided in the same courts, from the humble magistrates court, right up to the House of Lords, has to decide any other legal question.

KENNEDY: Yes. One of the things that fascinates me in a debate about a Bill of Rights, and so on, Lord McCluskey, is that, following on from what the Lord Chancellor says, that some of our constitutional provisions are just part of the Common Law. But to move to another point, the assumption is in your hostility to a Bill of Rights, is that it's going to be the present judiciary in its present form, which will administer it. Is there not an argument to say that if you have a different type of Court, differently constituted, that might meet some of your objections that the judges are only lawyers who are a little bit older?

MCCLUSKEY: There is an argument about that, but it worries me even more. If we are going to have a Bill of Rights, let our present judges look after it. I am terrified at the thought that someone selects and someone trains people to be special judges on human rights. I would rather that we used such judges as the system produces. Maybe we have to produce different judges, and I don't want to tempt the Lord Chancellor into an explosion on that.

SCARMAN: Can I intervene? I agree with you Lord McCluskey on that. I would trust our judges. I would always look to the education of our judges, and what is not often enough said, is that there has been a revolution in legal education since the war. Before the war I saw something of legal education at our universities, and what I saw, I didn't like. Legal education since the end of the war has been developing, and on the whole, developing admirably and particularly in bringing the lawyer into touch with other disciplines, medicine, sociology, and so forth. I have little doubt that our judges today, particularly the younger members of the High Court bench are as fine a corps of English judges as there has ever been.

KENNEDY: Lord Chancellor?

HAILSHAM: I do agree with both of the two last points. The constitutional law of America, where they have special courts, or a special Supreme Court, indicates the danger which McCluskey's pointing out, because if anyone looks at the way their main Chief Justice has recently been appointed, and the kind of grilling he was put through by members of Congress, it absolutely horrified me. What Lord Scarman says about the education of judges is true. We used to rely solely on in-service training, but now we do not, and I do think that the Board of Judicial Studies which is the core of our educational system for judges, is doing a very good job of work.

SCARMAN: But let me add one thing. The faculties of law, of British universities, have played a cardinally important, and very refreshing part, in improving legal institutions.

KENNEDY: May I take us to another subject? Lord McCluskey, something which features very significantly in one of your lectures is your commitment to the jury as an institution. You pick up the words of Lord Devlin that it's the 'lamp of freedom', and you say that if there were a tyrant, if not the first, the second thing he or she would do would be to get rid of the jury. Where does your commitment to the jury as an institution come from?

MCCLUSKEY: Well first of all from my direct experience both as a judge and as a practitioner. I've a lot of jury experience. Now as a judge, I know the immense difficulty that I have in almost every case where real questions of credibility come up for decision, and yet they have to be decided. And I would place much more faith in the judgment of 12 as in England, or 15 as in Scotland, people who come in off the street, and listen and judge what they hear, calibrated as it were against their own experiences of life. There's another point, too, and that is this: It is very difficult for any human being – even a judge – not to become prejudiced. He cares about certain things, he's against certain things and he's for certain things. There is no such thing as a prejudiced jury. It exists once; it delivers one verdict and it disappears. And although you may think that juries are prejudiced for plaintiffs in reparation actions, or against policemen in certain types of things; well you may think that if you like, but there's no such thing as a prejudiced jury. There's another thing, too that I believe that we in a sense patronise juries; we assume they're too stupid to understand, and we lay things out before them in a way that makes life unnecessarily complicated for ourselves. So I've a lot of faith in them, and I've a lot of experience of them, and it's my impression that juries do understand. I don't always agree with their verdicts, but that's another thing.

KENNEDY: Of course we know recently that there's been an argument that in very complicated fraud cases for example, juries simply can't understand what's going on and it's probably better to dispense with them. This was the argument in Lord Roskill's Report. Lord Chancellor, do you have any comment on that?

HAILSHAM: Well I'm half way between Devlin and Roskill, as it were. I have a great admiration in the same way as McCluskey has for trying a criminal case. But when my father went to the Bar (which was about 1903) almost everything was decided by jury. And in the last 85 years or so things have changed, and we now only try a very limited range of cases by juries. I think they are a bit unpredictable, and I don't agree that there is no such thing as a prejudiced jury. I do agree that it's a great advantage that they disappear and are never heard of again as a corporate body. But having said that, I don't think the point about complicated frauds has really been taken. A jury system will work only so long as you can get a random sample. Now supposing you're going to take a case – and never mind whether it's a fraud or anything else– which is going to take nine months sitting every day of the week except Saturdays and Sundays, where are you going to find your random jury? You're not finding a random sample, and it must follow from that that you must devise a better way of doing things. The very extent of international frauds of the most complicated kind. It's no criticism of juries to say that they don't understand double entry accounts, or laundering through Swiss banks and so on. What you can say with certainty – not because they don't understand it; they may understand it for aught I know, better than I do. But you can say that they are not a random sample because only those who've got nine months of their time to give (and they're not everybody) can possibly try the case at all.

KENNEDY: Of course we may encounter an echo of our conversation about Bill of Rights here. If it be argued that right to trial by jury is a basic human right which would be in a Bill of Rights, Lord Scarman, how would we deal with the sort of recommendations of Lord Roskill? Or indeed, the situation of the Diplock Courts in Northern Ireland?

SCARMAN: Well I think it would be wise not to complicate this discussion by reference to the Diplock Courts in Ireland. Both the Lord Chancellor and I have direct experience of the Irish situation, and they were ad-hoc, for a specific purpose connected with the terrorism out there, and I would much rather not comment. May I say this: I would only go along with a Diplock Court if there was an emergency situation which made it necessary. And I'm sure that this was Lord Diplock's view because I was in touch with him at the time he was considering all that. Now the other point, the Roskill point. I would retain juries for complex fraud cases. I would accept enthusiastically the Roskill proposals for more pre-trial work by the judge who is going to have the conduct of the case, so as to eliminate as much as possible which is not in issue, and so as to simplify those matters that are in issue. Of course the facts are bound to be complex, but that does not mean that the ultimate issue may not be a very simple one. Was something done or not done, fraudulent or deceitful or dishonest? And the skill of the judge, of course, is using the Roskill proposals for pre-trial work, and using his skill and experience in the trial to bring the jury through these complexities to a very simple question. And I believe most criminal cases should be able to be resolved. Therefore I would retain the jury because I still think in criminal cases *vox populi* must determine what is dishonest, what is wrong and what is not, and the jury is the only *vox populi* we've got.

KENNEDY: There is some unanimity here in that none of you are in favour of – using Lord McCluskey's works – trimming the wick of the lamp of freedom a great deal. But to pick up your point about *vox populi*, one thing that Lord McCluskey does propose, is it not, is that juries should be involved not only in verdicts of guilty or not guilty, but also in sentencing? What's your response, Lord Scarman, to that?

SCARMAN: That, if Lord McCluskey will allow me to say so, troubles me immensely. I think that the very random character of juries in most cases is a simple indication of how wrong this proposition is. A very important element – not the only element, but a very important element – in the administration of the criminal law is consistency in sentencing, subject to the particular circumstances of one case and another. If you're going to have a once-off tribunal determining sentence in cases, how can you enforce, other than by some elaborate appeal process, consistency between one jury's sentence and another in the same area of the law? And I think the argument based on consistency is enough to show that the jury is an inappropriate body to decide upon a sentence.

MCCLUSKEY: I wonder. You see, consistency is a virtue, but it is not an overriding virtue, and if you want to guarantee consistency, then you can have – as they have in some parts of the United States – presumptive sentencing. So you say to the jury you cannot award more than five years, but you can award as little as one year. And so you determine a range for the jury, and the jury come in and you get the feeling as to what the public really think about sentencing. Now before the discussion began, if the Lord Chancellor will permit me, he said that many people – members of the public – they want to hang and they want to castrate and cut off the hands of thieves and things like that. My experience is that that may be what people in the street think about crimes they read about in the papers, but once they come into court and they sit for several days, or even several weeks, they see the accused person, listen to the evidence, they discover the multi-faceted aspects of the case. Then they emerge as rational, judgmental human beings, and not people who are screaming for the scaffold. I think that the present system works very badly. You see, we are really ignoring the fact that by and large criminal judges in this country – including judges in the High Court both north and south of the Border – have very little criminal experience, have really no particular notion about what sentences are appropriate. They take their guidance from the Court of Appeal in each country, but who's the Court of Appeal? That's just some older judges who come from the same stable ultimately. And I think that in a sense judges don't really know what they're doing. And finally, if I may finish on this one note, it doesn't actually work.

HAILSHAM: Well, to be quite honest, this is a point on which I come down heavily against Lord McCluskey. I think sentencing is a most difficult art to begin with. As Lord Scarman was saying a moment ago in a slightly different context, there's been a revolution in judicial education. That is to say, what these judicial seminars are largely about is sentencing. Lord McCluskey's remedy is apparently to take away from those who have insufficient experience of sentencing, and give it to people who've got none, and disappear after one case. This seems to me to be an effort of logic which I'm not capable of following. It's all very well to talk about things like murder where the sentence is mandatory, or cases where there are clear cut guidelines. But how can a member of the jury taken off the street from the voting list, know the various non-custodial options which are the very stuff of which modern sentencing is made. Now I can tell McCluskey – because he referred to something I said just as we met before this discussion – that I get a postbag. For some reason people think that the Lord Chancellor has something to do with sentencing policy. He has nothing to do with sentencing policy. But I can tell you what the public is saying from the letters which Members of Parliament send on to me. They say the judges are much too lenient. The facts show, of course, that we pursue a much more severe sentencing policy than any other country in Western Europe. And there is a defect in our sentencing system, and that is that the Court of Appeal can only issue guidelines, and cannot in fact view a particular sentence alleged to be too lenient, in the context or the matrix of a particular set of facts. It can only argue about cases where the sentence is alleged to be too severe. And that, I think, is one of the reasons why the public have a false conception of what is going on. But the idea that you should take it away from the only people with any experience and give it to people with none, who disappear after one case, seems to me to be so paradoxical as to be illogical.

MCCLUSKEY: Yes, I can understand that simple point. But what I also say in the lecture – though I'm afraid I had to say it rather briefly – is that in a sense you have to educate the sentencing body in the particular case. And therefore you have to contend before the jury for the particular options or the length of sentence and so on, and you make it an open issue. At the moment we talk about sentencing policy, but there isn't one really. There's a kind of review by the Courts of Appeal, and that's all there is to it. And the judicial training that Lord Hailsham talks about is very short. And anecdotally people tell me who've been (and I haven't myself been) is that what happens basically is they all disagree about what the sentence would be in particular examples that they're given. That's my own experience of actual cases.

KENNEDY: There are precedents elsewhere, are there not, for the court to go into a sentencing phase after the verdict has been delivered?

MCCLUSKEY: I think that there ought to be a sentencing phase in those cases where the jury determines guilt, then the jury ought to go into a sentencing phase. And of course that happens in the United States, particularly in capital cases where they decide between the death penalty or life imprisonment; in rape cases where they decide between the same two options. So juries go into a sentencing phase. And I think that we would educate ourselves as well as the juries in going into this particular phase.

KENNEDY: May I take you to another matter? In your lectures you make a series of concrete proposals as well as your observations on the grander themes of law, justice and democracy. For example you ask; what should judges be doing (having disposed of the notion that they should be interpreting a Bill of Rights)? And you say well they should be solving the litigants' issues as they come up day by day, and that there are a number of obstacles in the way: delay, cost and the complexity of the law are the three that you mention. And you make some concrete proposals, one of which is the intriguing 110-day rule in Scotland.

MCCLUSKEY: Well in short, the 110-day rule which has obtained in Scotland since 1701, is that no person may be imprisoned for more than 110 days without being brought to trial. Now I know you're experimenting in England with similar limits.

SCARMAN: We're beginning to experiment.

MCCLUSKEY: . . . Beginning to experiment. But, what I think you have to do is you set up the limit first and then people will adapt to it. Just as when you say to people if you want to apply for shares in British Gas you must do it by Thursday the 14th. And if you don't do it by Thursday the 14th at 12 noon or whatever, that's the end of the matter. Well so it ought to be, I think in criminal cases. Because you can have cases in which the persons are in custody for a very, very long time before trial. There's a case in America at the moment where someone who has not yet been brought to trial has been in custody for three years awaiting trial.

SCARMAN: Lord McCluskey, I think the Scottish rule is an admirable rule. I'm glad we're experimenting, and I hope we shall get closer to the Scottish practice than at present looks likely. And therefore I have nothing further to add on that. I would like, if I might, just to revert for a moment to sentencing. I understand a point which I think your lectures are making, which is a good point and we mustn't overlook. Namely it's a case for greater lay participation in the sentencing process. I can see a powerful argument for that, but I don't think the jury is the correct mechanism for introducing the layman. We do have a practice in England. In the old days of the Quarter Sessions lay justices sat and assisted in sentencing, and in the Crown Court this also happens on occasions. I think, we could make use of our lay justices – if they were prepared to do it, because it's a very arduous task – to assist Crown Court judges in some classes of cases on sentencing. And I believe that this would allay a good deal of criticism that our sentencing is too much in the hands of a very tiny group of men and women.

HAILSHAM: Well of course, as has been said, we're experimenting in England on the kind of time limits set by Scotland for many years. I have much more reservations about it than either Lord Scarman or Lord McCluskey. Let me say first of all, I'd like to see some hard evidence that the delays were due to undue protraction by the prosecution. I have not seen any. Now the second thing I would like to say is if I were defending a client, I should find means of protracting the period until the trial became impossible. I don't think it would be very difficult. And the third thing I would say is that the big fish would get out and the little fish would be caught in the net. The big fish – people who've laundered their fradulent gains, or entered into a vast conspiracy of insider dealing will take months and months and months to evaluate. And they do. I am absolutely horrified at the thought that they would escape simply because 110 days was fixed for the time of investigation.

MCCLUSKEY: No no no . . .

HAILSHAM: . . . I think they should be punished, and they must be held because otherwise they'd go to Brazil before you caught them.

KENNEDY: Do big fish escape in Scotland?

MCCLUSKEY: No of course not.

HAILSHAM: You don't have so many as we do.

SCARMAN: But they do in Glasgow, with respect.

MCCLUSKEY: No, the 110-day rule is a rule against *imprisonment* awaiting trial. Accordingly, if a trial cannot be brought within the 110 days, then the person cannot be detained in prison. And there are very few fraud trials in which you would keep the person accused of fraud in prison. There is a 12-month rule which requires persons to be brought to trial within 12 months of the service of petition as it's called.

KENNEDY: One of the proposals you make, Lord McCluskey, to deal with problems such as, delay whereby the judge cannot do his job because there are so many cases pending hearing, is, in the context of crime, to suggest that there ought to be an amnesty for those charged with, let us say, not wicked crimes, whereas the wicked ones should still be prosecuted. That seems to me rather a dramatic proposal.

MCCLUSKEY: Well it may be. But at the moment we have both sides of the border an enormous backlog of cases, and we have to think how we can solve that problem. Now at the moment I know, as any lawyer knows—and I was the Public Prosecutor in Scotland for a while – I know that we in fact amnesty a number of cases. We may decide to prosecute people for careless driving if, but only if they exceed 50 miles an hour. We may, as we did with the strike of Civil Servants in Scotland some years ago, decide to amnesty a whole lot of people because we couldn't process the cases through the courts. In fact, at the moment we divert cases from the courts in various ways. Now I think that this practice, therefore, already exists, although its rather amorphous and not very formalised. And I believe, that we could, in fact make some decision in Parliament about those cases which could be amnestied to clear the backlog, and let's get down to bringing cases to justice as quickly as possible. Because that is also important, that people should be brought to a criminal court if they're going to be charged, as soon as may be.

HAILSHAM: Well nobody is more conscious of the dangers of delay than I am. But I think you must recognise the actual facts which is that the delays are due to the increase in serious crime. Fifteen per cent last year, average ten per cent compound interest over the last ten or more. And obviously the only rational answer to that is more courts and more judges. To let people off arbitrarily by an executive decision is not the rule of law or due process of law. Now there are various suggestions made both in civil and criminal procedure, which would involve a greater degree of judicial involvement. Perhaps I'm not the person to pontificate about that because I've never been a judge of first instance like the other two. But I do myself favour a cautious move in that direction, particularly in the Roskill cases, the serious fraud cases. But I am a little apprehensive of the prosecuting authority saying oh it's too much bother to prosecute this man although he's guilty, and to make up their minds as to who is a serious offender in advance. I think we've really got to get at the causes of crime, reduce the volume of crime, and adjust our judicial system so that there are adequate courts to deal with crime. I don't like amnesty on those lines.

KENNEDY: Lord McCluskey, may I, in the tradition of the Reith Lectures, give you the last word, and put to you if I may, a provocative comment? It seems to me that you have a view of the judge's role as a rather limited one, that his job is to get on and handle cases between litigants and leave important issues of policy to others. Would that be a fair appraisal?

MCCLUSKEY: Well I would prefer to put it at length – and I did in the Reith Lectures. But yes, I think that judges essentially, because they are not ultimately accountable, because of their background, ought to do the thing at which they're extremely good – deciding the issue before them. And they should be very hesitant about launching out onto the broad sunny uplands of human rights and natural law.

KENNEDY: Thank you, gentlemen, very much indeed.

NOTES

1 THE CHILL AND DISTANT HEIGHTS

1 This is the phrase used by Benjamin Cardozo in 'The Nature of the Judicial Process', Yale University Press, to describe, 'the realms of pure reason, above and beyond the sweep of perturbing forces', adding that Judges, 'do not stand aloof on these chill and distant heights; and we shall not help the cause of truth by acting and speaking as if they do.' See also R. E. Megarry, *Miscellany-at-law* (Stevens, 1955), Chapter 1.

2 Quoted (p. 4) by Woodward & Armstrong, *The Brethren* (Simon and Schuster, New York), from an address to the Ohio Judicial Conference in September, 1968.

3 In the House of Lords, Lord Wheatley, then Lord Justice-Clerk, speaking about devolution, said, '. . . we assume an elective silence on the political issues and confine ourselves, if we intervene at all, to constitutional or legal questions or views on practical matters affecting the law and its administration . . .'. (HL Deb, Vol. 367, col. 837 (January 27, 1979)). Others have been more forthcoming, eg Lord Hewart, then Lord Chief Justice, in 'The New Despotism' (1929). Lord Scarman, *English Law – The New Dimension*, 1974 Hamlyn Lectures (Stevens & Sons, 1974), and the contributions to the devolution debate by Lord Kilbrandon, then a Lord of Appeal in Ordinary and Chairman of the Royal Commission on the Constitution, 1969–73 cf. Cmnd. 5460, and HL Deb, Vol. 367, col. 795, (January 27, 1976).

4 Lord Denning, surprisingly, argues that 'it is a mistake to think of a Judge has having power', *Judges and the Judicial Power*, (Ed. Rajeev Dhavan, Sweet & Maxwell, 1986). The assertion is an unexpected one from a judge who exercised an enormous individual influence on the law and, therefore, on the rights of the citizen.

5 Appeal Courts can seldom be persuaded to take a different view of the facts, *Thomas* v. *Thomas*, 1947 SC (HL) 45, per Viscount Simon, p. 47.

6 *Donoghue* v. *Stevenson*, 1932 SC (HL) 31; [1932] AC 562.

7 *McColl* v. *Strathclyde Regional Council*, 1983 SLT 616.

8 Water (Fluoridation) Act 1985.

9 *Gillick* v. *West Norfolk and Wisbech Area Health Authority* [1985] AC 112.

10 See, for example, article by Simon Lee in *The Times*, March 13, 1986, 'Now the DHSS, GMC, and BMA are all in the business of issuing guidance which they think fit as in the Gillick context of contraception for teenagers.'

11 The first 'Brandeis brief' was submitted to the Supreme Court by Louis B. Brandeis (later an Associate Justice) as counsel in *Muller* v. *Oregon*, 208 US 412(1907). It was designed to present not just the law but the factual context in which the law fell to be

operated. Thus it set forth at great length the facts (or some facts) in relation to the employment of women in industry, and the Court decided to 'take judicial cognizance of all matters of general knowledge'. These matters included, 'the fact that woman has always been dependent upon man'. Even, 'a widespread and long continued belief concerning (a fact)' was 'worthy of consideration'. The brief contained extracts from legislation obtaining in various countries, and from over ninety reports of committees, 'bureaus (sic) of statistics', Commissioners of Hygiene and the like, from Europe as well as from the USA, to show that long hours of work were dangerous to women, 'because of their special physical organisation'. One has to wonder whether such a patronising excursus would be presented by women and by womens' organisations today!

12 *Rookes* v. *Barnard* [1964] AC 1129.

13 The Trade Disputes Act 1965 was enacted to 'restore' the law, according to Government spokesman in Parliament, c.f. the commentary by G. H. L. Fridman in Current Law Statutes, 1965.

14 In *Gouriet* v. *U.P.W.* [1977] QB 729 at pp. 736/7 Lord Denning asked: 'Are the Courts to stand idly by? . . . is the absence of the consent of the Attorney General a bar to anything being done, so that the courts are powerless to enforce the law?' The House of Lords, reversing the Court of Appeal, answered 'Yes', and held that only the Attorney General could sue on behalf of the public for the purposes of preventing public wrongs. This is a special case but it illustrates the general point that a court in the United Kingdom has to wait until the point of law is raised in a real dispute in the correct form and by parties who have an interest and a title to have the dispute adjudicated.

15 The citizen, even the journalist, is not to be blamed for not studying the reasoning. It is usually dense and technical as well as lengthy. Thus, for example, in *Rookes* v. *Barnard* the full reports of the arguments and opinions take up 181 pages. Other examples include the *Gouriet* case (referred to below) extending to 160 pages, and *Bromley L.B.C.* v. *Greater London Council* [1983] 1 AC 768 (the 'Fares Fair' case), reported in 85 pages. These examples are by no means exceptional.

16 Quoted at p. 191 by Alan Paterson in *The Law Lords* (Macmillan, 1982) from Lord Macmillan's *Law and other Things*. Paterson discusses the whole question under the heading 'The freedom to choose', and records the views of many eminent judges, including Lord Devlin, 'In each case you have a choice' and Lord Denning '. . . (in) . . . most cases you have got a choice . . . I go by policy and social considerations'. What is plain is that the Law Lords themselves take widely varying views as to the degree to which their decisions are inevitably compelled by the existing law.

17 See Cardozo, *The Nature of the Judicial Process* (Yale University Press, 1924) 'hardly a rule of today but may be matched by its opposite of yesterday.'

18 This was the expression used by Sir John Donaldson MR in *Secretary of State for Defence* v. *Guardian Newspapers* [1984] Ch. 156 at 165 in saying it was 'blindingly obvious' that national security required the identification of 'untrustworthy servants in a position to mishandle highly classified documents passing from the Secretary of State for Defence to other ministers'. Lord Scarman, in the House of Lords, ([1985] AC 339 at 346/5) concluded that 'the evidence fell far short of what was needed to establish that disclosure of the source of information was necessary in the interests of national security . . . it by no means follows that because a document is restricted to a limited high level

circulation its 'leak' to a newspaper will constitute a risk to national security . . . though a breach of trust by a Crown servant is (serious) . . . it does not, however, necessarily follow that national security has been endangered . . . the Court of Appeal thought the link 'blindingly obvious'. I do not; nor did Scott J.' Lord Fraser of Tullybelton took the same view as Lord Scarman.

19 *Donoghue* v. *Stevenson, supra.*

20 Lord Anderson in *Mullen* v. *Barr & Co.* 1929 SC 461 at 479, approved by Lord Buckmaster in *Donoghue* v. *Stevenson* at p. 43 in 1932 SC (HL).

21 Lord Atkin in *Donoghue* v. *Stevenson supra* p. 57.

22 Lords Buckmaster and Tomlin.

23 In *Reg.* v. *Sang* [1980] AC 402, a most important case about the admissibility of evidence in criminal trials, Lord Fraser of Tullybelton saw no cause for anxiety in the fact that discretion opens the door to subjectivity and variation as between different judges (p. 450).

24 The prosecutor confines himself to giving the judge details about the accused, such as age, marital status, employment record (sometimes), and lays before the court some record of the accused's previous convictions. He scrupulously avoids any elaboration about the wickedness of the offence or the state of public opinion and, unless invited to give assistance on technical matters, makes no suggestion as to the appropriate sentence. He is usually able, if asked to do so, to explain how any other persons involved in the same crime have been dealt with by another court.

25 HL Deb, Vol. 478, col. 160 (July 8, 1986 Lord Denning asked, 'Is the Minister aware that the extension of parole means that in many cases the sentences imposed by judges are rendered quite illusory?' The matter is fully discussed in the speech by Lord Scarman in *In re Findlay* [1985] AC 318 in which he refers to the legislation which empowers the Secretary of State to reduce longer sentences by two-thirds (under the parole system) but leaves him free not to do so. He 'has a complete discretion whether or not to accept the [Parole] Board's recommendation . . . neither the Board nor the Judiciary can be as close, or as sensitive, to public opinion as a minister responsible to Parliament and to the electorate.'

26 An appeal court will not alter a sentence imposed by the trial judge just because the trial judge has imposed a sentence different from that which the appeal court thinks is appropriate. He is allowed a margin of discretion. Only when he has gone seriously and obviously wrong will the appeal court interfere, unless it has new facts to go on. The Criminal Division of the Court of Appeal and its predecessors have sought to 'harmonise' sentencing c.f. Thomas, *Principles of Sentencing* (2nd ed. Heinemann), Chapter 1. This gave rise to 'tariff' sentencing, the sentence being primarily related to the offence, not to the offender or the prospects of his rehabilitation. In Scotland, the High Court of Justiciary does not attempt to prescribe a 'tariff'.

27 It is an understatement to say that prisons are full. They are seriously overcrowded: cf. *Prison Statistics, England and Wales*, 1985 (HMSO, Cmnd 9903), paras 10 and 11, Chapter 1; *Prisons in Scotland, Report for 1985* (HMSO Cmnd. 1, 1986) para. 6. The numbers detained in prison rise steadily and apparently inexorably.

28 In Appendix 3 of *The Sentence of The Court, a handbook for Courts on the Treatment of Offenders* (HMSO, March 1986) the average cost of custody per offender per week, for 1982/3, is given as £218. In high security/prisons for males the cost was £433 per week. The school fee for Oppidans at Eton in 1983 was £1,500 per term; and there was an entrance fee of £75. There is no entrance fee at HM Prisons.

29 In 1985 only about 13 *per cent* of the prison population in male prisons were receiving vocational or trade training or other educational courses. Twenty nine *per cent* of males were 'unoccupied': *Prison Statistics, England and Wales, 1985*. (Cmnd. 9903. Table 10). Sixty *per cent* of males are reconvicted within two years of discharge from prison after serving a sentence for a criminal offence: Chapter 8 of *Prison Statistics, England and Wales, 1985* (Cmnd. 9903. Tables 8(a) and (b)).

30 In *The Sentence of the Court* (1986 produced by the Home Office we find, chapter 3, p. 6, 'The research evidence . . . suggests that within the realistic range of choice, imposing particular sentences, or particularly severe sentences, has a very limited effect on crime levels', 'there is . . . no clear evidence associating sentence severity in crime rates.' (para. 3.4, p. 7) '. . . the perceived severity of the ensuing penalties has little effect. No evidence has been found that longer sentences or longer periods of incarceration produce better results than short sentences' (Sentence of the Court, 1978 Edition). In *Law and Order*, (Stevens, 1985), Ralf Dahrendorf, at p. 132, summarising 'the scepticism with regard to the effect of punishment which pervades the literature,' says, 'The death penalty does not deter murderers, and prisons do not deter thieves. Thirty years of detention do not 'improve' a person any more than five, and the cases in which detention of a particular person actually protects many others from injury, are rare.' Though he seems to argue that harsher sentences may be needed to increase 'a sense of institutional responsibility.'

31 Some judges think they do know the causes of crime. Thus, Lord Goddard, then Lord Chief Justice, said in 1952, 'Those who sit in the criminal courts know that it (human nature) does not change very much, and must come to the conclusion that the age-old causes of crime are still the desire for easy money, together with greed, passion, lust and cruelty'. Quoted by Anthony Mockler in *Lions Under The Throne* at pp. 281–2.

32 'Legislative Policy (insofar as it is expressed in statutory maxima) has, however, relatively little influence in the Court because maximum sentences . . . are in most cases far in excess of what the Court is normally prepared to uphold.' (Thomas, *Principles of Sentencing* (1970) p. 37). Of the Court of Appeal, he writes (at page XLVI) 'It is almost true to say that the policy and principles of the Court have developed as an oral tradition among the judges who sit upon the Court.'

33 Relatively few cases go to trial before a jury; but there are enough to allow juries to give a clear indication as to what the public consider to be appropriate sentences for common crimes. At the present time judges, whose contacts with the general public are extremely limited, have no reliable way of knowing what the public think about sentencing levels. Leaders in newspapers or utterances by spokesmen for particular interest groups, such as The Police Federation, cannot be regarded as authoritative guides to public opinion and attitudes. It is possible that juries might be more severe than judges; but it is by no means certain. Juries which have heard all the evidence are much more likely to make a considered and informed judgment than are citizens who are stopped in the street and asked to express off-the-cuff views to professional

opinion-gatherers. The legislature could, from time to time, pass presumptive sentencing statutes. In *The Massachusetts Courts, 1984, Annual Report* Chief Justice Hennessy describes the comprehensive presumptive sentencing Bill passed by the Massachusetts House of Representatives: presumptive sentencing entails the establishment by statute of an authorized maximum-minimum sentencing range for specified crimes, and, for each crime, a presumptive sentencing range within the maximum-minimum range. Such a system would compel the legislature to think closely about sentencing in the light of reliable indications from juries of public feeling. It could also lead to the development of procedures whereby evidence would be put before juries before they came to their sentencing decisions. Under the present system the thinking behind sentencing is obscure. Marcel Berlins, in *The Times'* profile of the Lord Chief Justice, Lord Lane, (November 28, 1985) states that the Lord Chief Justice refused to allow Judges to co-operate in an important and respectable academic study of sentencing policy. He is said to have 'considered that taking part in the research would be time consuming, achieve nothing, and could make the judges look foolish.' c.f. also p. 189 in Chapter 10, 'Refurbishing The Judicial Service', by Carol Harlow, *Public Law and Politics* (Sweet & Maxwell, 1986). Juries play some role in sentencing in the United States in some States in the most serious cases. For an example of a jury imposing the death penalty for rape, under Arkansas law, see *Maxwell* v. *Bishop*, 398 US 262 (1969/70), where it was affirmed that it was impermissible to remove jurors because they voice (in the *voir dire*) general objections to the death penalty or expressed conscientious or religious scruples against its infliction. See also *Witherspoon* v. *Illinois*, 391 US 510 (1967/8) relating to the role (and selection) of jurors in Illinois in imposing the death sentence in murder cases; the trial judge said early in the jury selection process – the *voir dire* – 'Let's get these conscientious objectors out of the way, without wasting any time on them', whereupon 47 potential jurors were successfully challenged because of their attitudes to the death penalty. The role of juries in deciding on the penalty in rape and murder cases in Georgia and Texas is also seen in the interesting case of *Furman* v. *Georgia*, 408 US 238 (1971/2) holding the death penalty to be a 'cruel and unusual punishment' in the circumstances of these cases. In Scotland a jury has the power to add a rider to a 'Guilty' verdict, and may thus exercise an ill-defined influence on the sentence imposed; but this happens rarely, and juries are seldom invited to play such a role. It is also well-known, of course, that the victim's concerns are largely left out of account. This is true at the state of passing sentence as well as earlier in criminal proceedings. So, for example, the discussion 'Help Victims – And Beat Crime' by John Spencer in *The Times*, March 5, 1986, which demonstrates the way in which the victims are 'often left completely in the dark,' 'After a guilty plea it is possible, and quite usual, for the defendant's lawyer to plead in mitigation of sentence that it was really the victim, not the defendant, who was to blame. . . . 'The victim cannot insist on being heard'. He quotes 'Victims in the Criminal Justice System' which demonstrates that victims though pleased with the police were 'increasingly disappointed with criminal justice as the case went on. By the end some were so fed up that they vowed that they would not bother to report an offence another time.'

34 Suggestions for the appointment of a Minister of Justice have come from many sources. Recent examples include 'Wanted: A Minister of Justice,' by the Rt Hon. David Steel, MP PC and Alex Carlile QC, MP in *Counsel*, (Trinity, 1986); Lord Gifford in Chapter 2 of *Where's the Justice?* (Penguin Books, 1986).

2 THE CLANKING OF MEDIEVAL CHAINS

1 'He is not a knight-errant, roaming at will in pursuit of his own ideal of beauty or of goodness', Cardozo, op. cit., p. 141.

2 See the thalidomide article written by the Editor of the *Sunday Times*, which gave rise to litigation both in the UK and in Europe. The article is quoted by Lord Reid in *Attorney-General* v. *Times Newspapers* [1974] AC 237 at 294.

3 For a critical and sceptical view of the history of attempts to achieve freedom of speech in the United States the reader is referred to the chapter by David Kairys, entitled 'Freedom of Speech' in *The Politics of Law* (David Kairys ed. Panther Books, New York, 1982). He concludes that, 'the ordinary person or group of ordinary persons has no means, based in the constitution or elsewhere, to engage meaningfully in that dialogue on the issues of the day that the First Amendment is so often heralded as promoting and guaranteeing . . . its reality is far less impressive than its rhetoric'. Mark Tushnet, in the chapter entitled 'Corporations and Free Speech' argues that Corporations dominate the media, that it is money that talks; and is equally gloomy about the contemporary reality of freedom of speech for the individual.

4 cf. *Nebraska Press Association* v. *Stuart*, 427 US 539 (1970) allowing pre-trial publication of potentially damaging information about a forthcoming murder trial.

5 'We should, I think, have regard to common sense, legal principle and public policy in that order.' Per Lord Reid in 'The Judge as Lawmaker' 12, Journal of the Society of Public Teachers of Law (1972) p. 22 at p. 25.

6 'The rules and principles of case law have never been treated as final truths, but as working hypotheses . . . The principles themselves are continually retested; for if the rules derived from a principle do not work well, the principle itself must ultimately be re-examined 'per Munroe Smith, *Jurisprudence* (Columbia University Press, 1909), p. 21, quoted by Cardozo, op. cit. p. 23.

7 *Donoghue* v. *Stevenson*, 1932 SC (HL) 31; [1932] AC 562.

8 *Hedley Byrne & Co.* v. *Heller & Partners* [1964] AC 465. See also *Haseldine* v. *Daw* [1941] 1 KB 458 (defectively repaired lift), *Junior Books Ltd* v. *The Veitchi Co. Ltd* [1983] AC 520; 1982 SC (HL) 244 (defectively constructed floor in a building).

9 *Donoghue* v. *Stevenson* (*supra*) at p. 42.

10 One who argues that development of the principle is not to the general advantage is Sir Henry Fisher in 'Law and Society' 1975, a lecture delivered before the Bar Association for Commerce, Finance and Industry on December 9, 1975, printed in the Minutes of Evidence taken before the *House of Lords' Select Committee on a Bill of Rights* (HMSO).

11 For an interesting description of some of the background of this case see *Lord Atkin* by Geoffrey Lewis (Butterworth; 1983) where the author shows how Lord Atkin enunciated the 'neighbour' principle two months before hearing the appeal.

12 347 US 483 (1954).

13 For a full account of the background to *Brown* v. *Board of Education*, see *The Unpublished Opinions of the Warren Court* by Bernard Schwartz, Chapt. 11 p. 445, Oxford University Press.

14 The opinions of the Scottish judges in the Court of Session have to be studied in *Mullen* v. *Barr & Co.*, 1929 SC 461, dealing with the same point.

15 *Gillick* v. *West Norfolk and Wisbech Area Health Authority* [1985] AC 112.

16 *Secretary of State for Defence* v. *Guardian Newspapers* [1985] AC 339.

17 *Albert* v. *Motor Insurers' Bureau* [1972] AC 301.

18 'An adequate theory of adjudication will recognize that in hard cases there are no correct legal answers. The judge must use his discretion in deciding between alternative solutions each of which is legally permissible.' (p. 50) in the Essay by David Pannick, in *Judges and the Judicial Power* (Ed. Rajeev Dhavan, Sweet & Maxwell, 1986).

19 The best sustained argument on this theme is *The Politics of the Judiciary*, by J. A. G. Griffiths (3rd ed. 1985, Fontana Press). See also, *Where's the Justice?* by Tony (Lord) Gifford QC (Penguin Books, 1986).

20 In 'The Judge as Law Maker' 12, Journal of the Society of Public Teachers of Law (1972) p. 22 Lord Reid said, 'The jurist may ask what I mean by law . . . the practical answer is that the law is what the judge says it is.' He also says 'There was a time when it was thought almost indecent to suggest that judges make law – they only declare it . . . but we do not believe in fairytales any more.'

21 S 2(1) of the Law Reform (Personal Injuries) Act, 1948, as amended by s 1(3) of the Social Security (Consequential Provisions) Act, 1975.

22 *Parry* v. *Cleaver* [1970] AC 1, in which (by a majority of 3:2) the House of Lords decided that a disablement pension, payable out of a police pension fund to a police constable who had made compulsory contributions to the fund, was to be left out of account in assessing the constable's financial loss resulting from a road accident in which he sustained severe injuries.

23 One of the most striking cases, and one of the most important in the development of judicial review, to illustrate this is *Anisminic* v. *Foreign Compensation Commission* [1969] 2 AC 147 where the House of Lords held that the Commission's decision was a nullity, despite a provision in an Act of Parliament that, 'The determination by the Commission of any application made to them under this Act shall not be called in question in any court of law.'

24 The common law of Scotland was derived from different sources from the common law of England. But the Union of 1707 allowed litigants to appeal from the Scottish Courts to the House of Lords in civil, though not criminal, cases. For assorted reasons many cases were appealed; it was not until well into the 19th century that the number of English appeals for the first time exceeded the number from Scotland. The 'Scotch' appeals were not decided by lawyers with any knowledge of Scots Law. So when Scots Law produced one answer to a legal question and English Law produced a different answer the House of Lords would usually apply the English rule to Scotland. This process continued into the 20th century, even after the arrival of Scottish judges in the House of Lords. When Parliament began to step in to alter a common law rule it tended to overrule the law derived from the English common law and to enact in its place the law that the Scottish common law had evolved. For a scholarly, eloquent and impassioned account of the influence of English law on Scots law, see T. B. Smith, *British Justice: The Scottish Contribution*, The Hamlyn Lectures 1961 (Stevens, 1961). In his

Inaugural Lecture on assuming the Chair of Civil Law at Edinburgh, Sir Thomas Smith said, 'Alas, since 1758, we in Scotland have gone awhoring after some very strange gods' The Juridical Review, 1959, p. 119 (W. Green & Son).

25 In Chap. 5 of The Politics of the Judiciary *op. cit.* Professor Griffith illustrates this reluctance, especially during the inter-war years; and, in relation to statutory powers to interfere with the common law property right of an individual, concludes, 'The idea that Parliament, in this field, was 'interfering' with the common law died hard' (p. 130). In reversing the Court of Appeal, and deciding in favour of the narrower construction of the Race Relations Act, 1968, the House of Lords was conscious of the fact that the Act was restricting a common law right to choose one's associates. Lord Diplock said (pages 295/6 of *Race Relations Board* v. *Dockers' Club* [1976] AC 285, 'This is a statute which, however admirable its motives, restricts the liberty which the citizen previously enjoyed at common law to differentiate between one person and another in entering or declining to enter into transactions with them. It falls to be construed within the framework of the general law relating to transactions between private citizens . . . The law cannot dictate one's choice of friends.' In *English Law: The New Dimension* (Stevens, 1974), Lord Scarman speaks of, 'the helplessness of the law in face of the legislative sovereignty of Parliament . . .' (p. 15) (note the interesting assumption that 'the law' is somehow violated or polluted by the enactments of a sovereign Parliament). Lord Devlin in The Judge (Oxford University Press, 1981) describes the judges' attitudes to parliamentary intrusions into the common law as follows (p. 15):

> 'In the past judges have been obstructive. But the source of the obstruction, it is very important to note, has been the refusal of judges to act on the ordinary meaning of words. They looked for the philosophy behind the Act and what they found was a Victorian Bill of Rights, favouring (subject to the observance of the accepted standards of morality) the liberty of the individual, the freedom of contract, and the sacredness of property, and which was highly suspicious of taxation. If the Act interfered with these notions, the judges tended either to assume that it could not mean what it said or to minimise the interference by giving the intrusive words the narrowest possible construction, even to the point of pendantry.'

26 Especially by Lord Denning on numerous occasions. See also the article by Robert Alexander QC, Chairman of the English Bar, in *The Times*, December 10, 1985, entitled 'Human rights: trust our judges'.

27 In the Denning Lecture (March 29, 1983) Lord Roskill said 'We have suddenly developed an entirely new system of administrative law . . . the change has been brought about almost entirely by the judiciary . . .'

28 *Reg.* v. *Secretary of State for the Environment, ex parte Nottinghamshire County Council* [1986] AC 240, at pp. 247/8.

29 *Gillick* v. *West Norfolk & Wisbech Area Health Authority* [1985] AC 112.

30 *Edwards* v. *Bairstow* [1956] AC *14; Secretary of State for Education and Science* v. *Tameside BC* [1977] AC 1014.

31 *Reg.* v. *Hillingdon London Borough Council, ex parte Puhlhofer* [1986] AC 484.

32 *O'Reilly* v. *Mackman* [1983] 2 AC 237.

33 This is particularly clearly in the *Gillick* case. It was not brought under the judicial

review procedure, but that did not trouble their Lordships. By the time the case reached the House of Lords the question was academic because the local Health Authority did not appeal against the declaration Mrs Gillick had obtained in the Court of Appeal; the Court overcame its reluctance to deal with academic questions and felt able to consider what Lord Bridge of Harwich described as, 'Mrs Gillick's crusade . . . against the ethos expressed in the memorandum . . . issued to all health authorities by . . . the Department of Health and Social Security'. But, most important, they felt able to entertain the case despite the fact that the memorandum issued by DHSS had 'no statutory force whatever. It is not and does not purport to be issued in the exercise of any statutory power or in the performance of any statutory function. It is purely advisory in character and practitioners in the National Health Service are, as a matter of law, in no way bound by it' (Lord Bridge of Harwich). It is difficult to avoid the conclusion that in a case which had attracted enormous public interest the House of Lords was reluctant to be seen announcing that, for technical reasons, it couldn't decide the case, particularly as the majority thought that the Court of Appeal had come to the wrong answer to the real underlying question. So perhaps the most enduring result of the *Gillick* case will not be its effect upon doctors and contraception but its effect in enlarging the jurisdiction of the Court in judicial review.

34 In his *in memoriam* note marking Lord Diplock's role in the area of administrative law, Lord Wilberforce shows how, after his judgment in *Anisminic* v. *Foreign Compensation Commission* [1968] 2 QB 862 was reversed by the House of Lords, [1969] 2 AC 147, Lord Diplock became progressive in developing the notion of 'public' law and in formulating the grounds for administrative review. 'In the whole of this area', writes Lord Wilberforce, 'we see a judicial legislator – cautiously – at work'. Public Law (Spring 1986) p. 6 Lord Diplock's speech in *CCSU* v. *Minister for the Civil Service* [1985] AC 374 gives some account to the development of judicial control of administrative action.

35 These are the expressions used by H. W. R. Wade in Constitutional Fundamentals (Stevens, 1980 Chap. 5.) He argues that judges should be more courageous in fighting what he conceives to be Parliament's abuse of legislative power' (p. 68). He regards British lawyers as 'brainwashed . . . by the dogma of legislative sovereignty . . .'

36 An Australian scholar arrives at the same conclusion as Professor Wade; referring to what he calls 'The Polite Rebellion', Professor G. De Q. Walker writes, 'In a line of cases beginning with *Anisminic Ltd* v. *Foreign Compensation Commission* the Courts have squarely, though with extreme courtesy and diffidence, disregarded the clear wording of Acts of Parliament . . . the courts have thus effectively rebelled against Parliament . . . The judges have almost given us a constitution, establishing a kind of entrenched provision to the effect that even Parliament cannot deprive them of their proper function': The Australian Law Journal, Vol. 59, May 1985, p. 276.

3 HARD CASES AND BAD LAW

1 That does not prevent Judges from criticising the language used by Parliament; but the Judges are careful to criticise not Parliament itself, but the draftsman; the monkey gets the blame for the organ grinder's music. R. E. Megarry has collected some examples in the final chapter of *Miscellany-at-law* (Stevens). A classic is the lament of Mackinnon LJ in *Winchester Court Ltd* v. *Miller* [1944] KB 734 at 744: 'He must be a bold, if not a conceited, man who can feel confidence in forming, or expressing, an opinion on any one of the innumerable problems that arise out or what may be cited together as the Rent

and Mortgage Interest Restrictions Act, 1920 to 1939, but, having once more groped my way about that chaos of verbal darkness, I have come to the conclusion, with all becoming diffidence, that the county court judge was wrong in this case. My diffidence is increased by finding that my brother Luxmoore has groped his way to the contrary conclusion.'

2 Scots Law has consistently rejected the idea of punitive or exemplary damages for personal injuries: cf. Lord President Dunedin in *Black* v. *North British Railway Co.* 1908 SC 444 at 453. The purpose of the law is accurately reflected in the name used in Scotland, 'Reparation'. English Law allows the payment of exemplary damages 'to punish and deter' but such awards are made only in special circumstances and in a very restricted range of cases: cf. the speech of Lord Devlin in *Rookes* v. *Barnard* [1964] AC 1129 at 1221 *et seq.* The possibility of awarding aggravating damages gives rise in England to considerable difficulties in applying the law cf. *Riches and Others* v. *Newsgroup Newspapers Ltd* [1985] 2 All ER 845 where the trial judge was held to have 'seriously misdirected' the jury on the issue of exemplary damages in a libel action by Banbury CID offices against the owners of the *News of the World*. In *Cassell & Co.* v. *Broome* [1972] AC 1027, Lord Hailsham, the Lord Chancellor, spoke of 'inextricable confusion'. English Courts do not award aggravated damages in medical negligence cases cf. *Kralj* v. *McGrath* [1986] 1 All ER 54, but some American Courts can and do.

3 It would be impossible to better, and pointless to repeat, the summary of the development of employers' liability law since 1837 given by John Munkman in *Employer's Liability at Common Law* (10th ed. Butterworths) Chap. 1, and Lord Atkin's speech in *Radcliffe* v. *Ribble Motor Services Ltd* [1939] AC 215. (Common Employment).

4 Statistics showing how few cases are fought to a finish can be found in the *Report of the Royal Commission on Civil Liability* (the Pearson Commission), Cmnd 7054–1. c.f. Chapters 3 and 18, vol. 2.

5 It is by no means impossible for Courts to develop positive regulatory powers by the technique of prohibiting the doing of some act or the carrying-on of some activity until steps prescribed by the Court have been taken. American Courts made many such orders in the field of civil rights, especially in relation to integration of schools and bussing. British Courts issue such orders, but not to compel employers to conduct their operations carefully.

6 Penal or aggravated damages may be awarded in some cases. The result is to inflate some awards of damages and most insurance premiums.

7 'American Culture Encourages Lawsuits.' Nicholas O. Berry, Chairman of the Political Science Department at Urfinus College, quoted in 22 ABA Journal, the lawyers' magazine. There are about 350,000 lawyers in America, which is, proportionately about three times as many as in the United Kingdom. The preliminary findings of the American Bar Foundation's research (reported, ABA Journal, August 1, 1986) suggest that public concern about punitive damages may be overdone, partly because the few huge awards draw undue attention. In some States punitive damages are not allowed at common law. In most the plaintiff has to prove some special factor, such as malice, wilful misconduct, fraud, before punitive damages can be awarded. Most such awards were not made in medical negligence or product liability cases. But the overall picture was very uneven. The percentage of jury awards containing punitive damages ranged

from 1% to 21.6%; and most plaintiffs tended to lose anyway. If the plaintiff did win and received punitive damages his award could be very high indeed; even in negligence cases. The effects upon negotiated settlements of the risks of such awards would be impossible to study successfully: insurance premiums reflect not just those cases in which the plaintiff wins in court but the cases which settle, and also those cases which the plaintiff loses in court; it costs a lot to win a case against an impecunious litigant.

8 In *Other Peoples Law* Lord Kilbrandon referred to the recovery of damages as a 'lottery' and the assessment of damages as a 'guess'. The whole civil jury trial he described as a 'degrading form of bingo-session'. This was said in 1966.

9 No-fault schemes have been introduced in Sweden, New Zealand, Canada, in some States in USA, and in parts of Australia.

10 This was done, for example, in the capital punishment cases. *Furman* v. *Georgia* (and other cases) 408 US 238 (1972).

11 In *The Judge*, p. 15.

12 Typical examples include *Donoghue* v. *Stevenson (supra)*, and *The Sunday Times* Thalidomide case: *Attorney-General* v. *Times Newspaper* [1974] AC 273.

13 This was the line of defence successfully advanced, in law, by a woman who had been apart from her husband for thirteen months before giving birth to a daughter: *MacLennan* v. *MacLennan* 1958 SC 105. But when she declined to give the details as to how, where and when she had been artificially inseminated her defence was repelled and she was divorced on the ground of her 'presumed' adultery.

14 Cardozo, in *The Nature of the Judicial Process* (p. 135) quotes Article 4 of the French 'code civil': 'The judge who shall refuse to give judgment under pretext of the silence, of the obscurity, or of the inadequacy of the law, shall be subject to prosecution as guilty of a denial of justice'. We avoid the embarrassing inconvenience of prosecuting judges by allowing them to find against the litigant who has failed to discharge the onus which the law places upon him; though, strictly speaking, that device applies only to the facts. A judge will always decide a question of law if he cannot avoid doing so. If he is tortured by doubt there is a stock of well-known phrases he can use to signal it.

15 cf. *Jamieson* v. *Jamieson* [1952] AC 525; 1952 SC (HL) 44, where the husband was merely alleged to be extremely selfish and inconsiderate; *Tullis* v. *Tullis* 1953 SC 312 where the wife was alleged to have 'nagged' her husband into impotence. The change in the law was completed in 1964 in *Gollins* v. *Gollins* [1964] AC 644 where the House of Lords, by a majority of three to two, held that intention to injure was not an essential ingredient of cruelty; and in *Williams* v. *Williams* [1964] AC 698 in which the same narrow majority decided that insanity was no defence to a charge of 'cruelty'. Parliament decided that the judges should stretch the concept of cruelty no further and provided instead the elastic notion of behaviour such that the other spouse cannot 'reasonably' be expected to 'live' with the respondent: Matrimonial Causes Act, 1973, s 1(2)(b) [England and Wales] Divorce (Scotland) Act, 1976 [Scotland], the only difference being the use, in the Scottish Act, of the word 'cohabit' instead of the word 'live.'

16 A good example is *Duncan* v. *Jones* [1936] 1 KB 218. Mrs Duncan, of the National Unemployed Workers' Movement, stepped onto a box to address a number of people in the street outside an 'unemployed training centre'. There was no obstruction and no one

present was alleged to have committed, incited or provoked any breach of the peace. But a police officer 'reasonably apprehended' that a breach of the peace would occur if she addressed the meeting at that spot. He told Mrs Duncan she could hold her meeting 175 yards away. She declined to go and started speaking from the box. She was arrested and duly found guilty of wilfully obstructing a police constable in the execution of his duty. On appeal, Humphreys J said it did not require authority (i.e. precedent) to emphasise the statement that 'it is the *duty* of a police officer to prevent apprehended breaches of the peace'. On this basis it is not entirely clear how the police can allow Chelsea FC to play Leeds FC or Rangers play Celtic. Another interesting example is recorded in *Alexander* v. *Smith* 1984 SLT 176. Alexander was trying to sell a National Front newspaper outside a football ground. Supporters on their way to a match, presumably incensed by Alexander's politics, shouted to the police that, unless they did something about it, there would be trouble, and one supporter knocked Alexander's hat off; but all these supporters entered the football ground. Alexander was not proved to have done anything except jump up and down shouting the name of the paper. The police, concerned that the situation might get worse and that Alexander himself might be injured, told him to 'move on'. He declined on the ground that he was doing nothing unlawful. The police seized him, took the papers from him and removed him; he shouted a protest. He was convicted of a breach of the peace. Those who uttered the threats were not arrested. If Alexander had been a member of the Salvation Army selling *War Cry* to the annoyance of passing atheists, on their way to an atheists' convention, one of whom had knocked his cap off, the situation in law would have been indistinguishable. So the practical effect of the law seems to be that if police officers form the view that a breach of the peace could develop because X might, on some future occasion, react unlawfully to Y's lawful behaviour, then the police have a right and a duty to put a stop to Y's lawful behaviour if he does not desist. Or, to put it another way, Y can be stopped from doing that which is lawful if X might react by doing that which is unlawful. It was, of course, this general state of the law which, in 1984, enabled the police to stop persons from driving along the public highway lest they join a lawful picket or demonstration fifty or a hundred miles away and, by swelling the numbers of pickets or protestors there, threaten a possible breach of the peace or 'obstruction'. The trouble with all such vague and ill-defined notions – whether it be 'anti-Soviet behaviour', 'obstruction', 'breach of the peace' or even 'bringing the game into disrepute' – is that they confer ill-defined powers and discretion upon those immediately responsible for policing the law. Courts are extremely reluctant to step in, even if they get the chance, and say that the police or others concerned with rule-enforcement have acted upon a misjudgment of what was reasonably to be apprehended. So the rule of law, which requires that no one shall be punished by a criminal court except for behaviour which is known to be criminal when it is engaged in, and which allows citizens to go about their lawful activities unmolested by the police, suffers a significant and imprecise abridgment. The right of the police to take such steps as they thought proper to avoid the risk, as they saw it, of a breach of the peace resulting from the presence of too many pickets was affirmed in *Riddington* v. *Bates et al* [1960] 3 All ER 660, DC, where the police officer decided that two pickets were enough to picket the back door of a factory. When a third, Bates, tried to join them he was arrested.

17 In *Radcliffe* v. *Ribble Motor Services Ltd.* [1939] AC 215, Lord Wright said that the doctrine of common employment was, 'an arbitrary departure from the rules of the common law based on a prejudiced and one-sided notion of what was called public

policy, and sanctioned by no previous authority'. Although all their Lordships regarded the doctrine as unloved they said it was too well-established to be overthrown by judicial decision; and then proceeded to disembowel it by holding that two motor coach drivers employed by the same company, one of whom knocked down and killed the other in the street, were not in common employment at the time. Curiously, the same Court breathed fresh life into the doctrine when they applied it in *Miller* v. *Glasgow Corporation* 1947 SC (HL) 12, [1947] AC 368 to prevent a tram conductress from recovering damages for injuries when her tram which was struck by another Corporation tram, the driver of which negligently failed to apply the brakes so that it collided with the tram in which she was the conductress. The significant point of fact causing her and the driver to be in 'common' employment appeared to be that both trams were running on the same set of rails. Now buses do not run on rails; so, six months later, in *Neilson* v. *Pantrini, and Glasgow Corporation* 1947 SC (HL) 64, [1948] AC 79, the conductress of a Corporation bus was held entitled to recover damages for injuries when her bus was struck by another Corporation bus the driver of which negligently failed to apply the brakes so that it collided with the bus in which she was the conductress; the buses though using a common route were *not* running on rails. Such nonsensical distinctions, all derived from *Hutchison* v. *York, Newcastle and Berwick Railway Co.* (1850) 5 Exch. 343, were consigned to the dustbin of history by The Law Reform (Personal Injuries) Act, 1948, despite the view expressed by Pollock CB of *Hutchison's* case that, 'there never was a more useful decision, or one of greater practical and social importance in the whole history of the law.' (cf. *Vose* v. *Lancashire and Yorkshire Railway Co.* [1858] 27 LJ Exch. 249 (at p. 252).

18 HMSO 1986.

19 [1986] 1 AC 455.

20 This summary of the judge's attempts to assist the jury, and their response, is borrowed from Lord Scarman's speech (pp. 470/1).

21 *R* v. *Maloney* [1985] AC 905.

22 In *Williams* v. *Florida*, 399 US 78 (1970) it was decided that six is a permissible number of jurors in a criminal case. The selection of twelve jurors was described as 'a historical accident'. Lord Coke's explanation that the 'number of twelve is much respected in Holy Writ as twelve apostles . . . twelve tribes etc.' was dismissed as 'typical' of 'fanciful reasons for the number twelve'. In Scotland there are fifteen jurors in a criminal case but their numbers may be reduced in the course of the case to twelve, as jurors may be excused on various grounds. In the Court of Session a civil jury consisted of twelve members; but in the Sheriff Court the number was seven, until civil jury trials in the Sheriff Court were abolished in 1980. In England, of course, the number is twelve in either a civil or a criminal case. For the origins of the jury system in England, see Devlin, *Trial by Jury*, 1956 Hamlyn Lectures (Stevens, 1956). Lord Morris of Borth Y Gest *Report of the Departmental Committee on Jury Service* 1965 Cmnd 2627. For Scotland see 'The Origins and Development of the Jury in Scotland' Stair Society (1966) Volume 23 Ian D. Willock.

23 E.g. in Canada, and, formerly, in England.

24 In Scotland, eight out of fifteen (or of fourteen, thirteen or twelve).

25 In England, ten out of twelve.

26 In parts of USA cf. *Maxwell* v. *Bishop; Furman* v. *Georgia (supra)*. In a current case, *California* v *Brown* (No. 85–1563) the Supreme Court is examining the role of the Jury in deciding between the death penalty and life imprisonment for a person convicted of rape and murder.

27 This is still true: cf. *Fraud Trials Committee Report* (Lord Roskill) HMSO 1986. The recommendation of Lord Morris's committee for jurors to be disqualified if unable to read and understand English has not been implemented: *Report of the Departmental Committee on Jury Service* (1965) Cmnd 2627.

28 At p. 105, Lord Kilbrandon refers to 'the notion, not uncomon to this day, that a criminal trial is a combination of ceremonial ritual and sporting event' *Other People's Law*, The 1966 Hamlyn Lectures (Stevens, 1965).

29 Lord Hailsham, speaking as Mr Quintin Hogg, MP, in 1966, 'When I look at the panoply of English criminal justice at assizes I am reminded of a foxhunt . . .'

30 The Devlin quotation is contained on p. 164 of *Trial by Jury*, the 1956 Hamlyn Lectures (Stevens, 1956), 'The first object of any tyrant in Whitehall would be to make Parliament utterly subservient to his will; the next to overthrow or diminish trial by jury . . . So that trial by jury is more than an instrument of justice and more than one wheel of the constitution: it is the lamp that shows that freedom lives.'

31 *Freedom under the Law* (Stevens).

32 The jury has remained much more relevant in the United States than in England and the Seventh Amendment guarantees its retention. Although there is no right to a jury trial before the State Courts more than 100,000 cases a year are decided by jury trials (that is civil cases).

33 The report of the Commission to consider legal procedures to deal with terrorist activities in Northern Ireland, Chairman Lord Diplock, (December 1972) is Cmnd 5185. It recommended replacement of jury trials by 'Diplock courts' principally because in ordinary trials the administration of justice was being prevented by intimidation by terrorist organisations. The 'Diplock courts' were set up by the Northern Ireland (Emergency Provisions) Act, 1973.

34 Lord Roskill's own tentative views were ventilated in the Denning Lecture on March 29, 1983. He said *inter alia*: 'Where I venture to think that drastic reforms are now required and a lot of hard re-thinking is necessary, is in the trial of cases of alleged commercial fraud . . . I have been wondering whether whatever the protests may be from the traditionalists we have not now reached the stage when these cases should be taken out of the ordinary system of criminal justice . . . and be tried in a special court . . . Perhaps a modified version of the old City of London Special Jury might be revived.'

35 In a memorandum recently set to MPs in relation to the proposed abolition of peremptory challenge to jurors the NCCL notes: 1967, abolition of the unanimous verdict; 1973, The right to question jurors restricted; substantial reduction in the types of cases sent for jury trial (including public order cases); 1977, defendants' right to peremptory challenge reduced to three (previously seven); 1978, jury vetting legitimised by the Attorney-General; and 1984, substantial increase in number of persons disqualified from sitting on juries. Section 23 of the Criminal Justice (Scotland) Act, 1980, reduced

the number of peremptory challenges from five to three. Clause 83 of the current Criminal Justice Bill provides for the total abolition, in England and Wales, of the right to challenge jurors without 'cause.'

36 In Scotland, in the vast majority of cases, unless Parliament has ordered that the offences must be tried by a judge sitting alone. The Lord Advocate, who is the public prosecutor, has a discretion as to whether a case is sent for trial by jury or for trial by a judge sitting without a jury.

37 See Ian Willock, 'The Jury in Scotland' (Stair Society, Volume 23, p. 222) in which he quotes the view of jurors expressed by Lord Advocate Mackenzie (1677–87 and 1688) 'Assizers with us are oftentimes ignorant persons'. In the Debate in the Houses of Lords on the Roskill Report on 10th February 1986 (Official Report, fifth series, Lords, Volume 471, column 55) Lord Denning having discussed the growth of complications in commerce and finance giving rise to opportunities for frauds said that fraud was a 'great modern disease' and added 'that is why I am afraid we have to leave trial by jury and we have to replace it by a modern instrument.' He contrasted unfavourably modern jurors with the jurors of fifty years ago, 'Jurors were not then any old chap on the voting list: they have to be householders . . . tradesmen . . . all male, all middle class and middle-aged, and they dealt with their cases splendidly, if I may say so . . . of course, we knew their occupations: they were bank clerks, insurance clerks and so on . . . now . . . they turn up in Court . . . youngsters of eighteen or nineteen, girls and boys, peoples of all sorts and descriptions . . . those are the kinds of people that you have.' Despite drawing attention to some unnecessary practices which resulted in the selection of some jurors who might be unfitted for the task, the committees referred to above and the committee sitting under Lord Strachan in Scotland (*Civil Jury Trial in Scotland*, Scottish Home Dept. Cmnd 851) found no persuasive evidence that juries were bad judges. There are, of course, some examples of juries that made serious mistakes. But it would not be difficult to compile a glossary of examples of error, prejudice and simple incompetence on the part of judges.

38 For Scotland, Gordon defines fraud at common law by reference to an authoritative text-book by McDonald as 'the bringing about of some definite practical result by false pretences' Chapt. 18, *The Criminal Law of Scotland*, by Gerald Gordon (2nd ed., 1978).

39 In the wake of the Roskill Report, that has been suggested, e.g. writing in *Counsel*, the journal of the Bar of England and Wales, Hilary, 1986, Lord Benson, a member of the Roskill Committee on Fraud Trials, says 'Common sense dictates that if changes are to be adopted in fraud cases some of them would be appropriate in all criminal procedures.' As he narrates, '. . . juries will need to be literate. This is not a requirement for jurors at present – instances came to our notice where jurors have been sworn who can barely read and write and in some cases cannot do either'.

4 TRUSTING THE JUDGES

1 If one of the parties (usually on the employers' side of the battle) brings an industrial dispute to Court it is almost invariably to seek an *interim* order. The Court cannot in the time available allow the case to be conducted in the same way as an ordinary litigation, for that could take years. It is very rare for the dispute to last for years. And when a dispute is settled, the litigation, along with its *interim* orders, disappears. But they may have played a decisive part in bringing one side or the other to its knees. Occasionally the case will survive the settlement of the dispute because the parties and the Court agree that

there is a point of law worth settling. A good example is *Express Newspapers Ltd* v. *McShane* [1980] AC 672 where the *interim* order was pronounced against officials of the NUJ by Lawson J on the basis that their defence would be unlikely to succeed. The Court of Appeal upheld the judge's order *Express Newspapers Ltd* v. *McShane* [1979] WLR 390. A year later, when the dispute was over and the order ineffective, the House of Lords unanimously ruled that the lower courts were both wrong, and that the order should be discharged. Had the order not been made in the first place the NUJ's bargaining position would certainly have been stronger.

2 I should not want to give the impression that all or even most judges are quite indifferent to the content of the law, though it is true that judges seldom resign in protest against some change in the law they have to apply, even in a revolutionary situation, such as occurred in Germany in 1933 or in Southern Rhodesia in 1965 and resulted in fundamental changes in the constitutional basis and validity of the legal order. It is in such situations that it becomes clearest that judges are non-political. They stay in office and apply the new laws.

3 Judges do not seek to conceal that they are making policy choices. In *McLoughlin* v. *O'Brien and Others* [1983] AC 410, a case involving negligence and the ambit of the duty of care, Lord Wilberforce said (p. 420) that at the margin the boundaries of a man's responsibility for acts of negligence have to be fixed 'as a matter of policy'. He acknowledges the making by judges of policy judgments in the whole field of judicial review of administrative action when he writes ('Public Law' [1986] PL 7, Spring 1986, p. 7) in praise of Lord Diplock's progressive formulation of the grounds for such review. Lawyers who have in recent years encountered such unfamiliar creatures as the 'doctrine' of '"legitimate expectation" . . . "proportionality" (not yet worked out) and the gloss of "irrationality" – that it must be outrageous, in defiance of logic and accepted moral standards' will have little difficulty in agreeing that judicial policy has changed since *Liversidge* v. *Anderson* [1942] AC 206, an embarrassing case whose unlamented demise has been pronouned e.g. by Lord Scarman: *Reg.* v. *Home Secy ex p. Khawaga,* [1984] 1 AC 74, and *Reg.* v. *IRC ex p. Rossminster* [1980] AC 952 at p. 1025. Lord Diplock added at p. 1071, 'I think the time has come to acknowledge openly that the majority in this House were expediently and at that time, perhaps, excusably, wrong . . .' In the devising of the 'principles' that set limits on the assessment and reduction of damages Lord Reid said on the bench what he later said in the article referred to above (The Judge as Law Maker), that the common law treated this matter as one 'depending on justice, reasonableness and public policy': *Parry* v. *Clearer* [1970] AC 1 at p. 13. In the criminal law too the judges make clear policy choices: a good example is *R. v Majewski* [1977] AC 443 where the question was whether a man who was out of his mind through self-induced intoxication fell to be acquitted of a crime (assault) of which *mens rea* was an essential ingredient. The House of Lords held he should not be acquitted. The Scottish Court arrived at the same conclusion (*Brennan* v. *HM Advocate* 1977 JC 38) saying the question had been resolved 'as a matter of legal policy to set, in the public interest, acceptable limits upon the circumstances in which any person may be able to relieve himself of criminal responsibility.' Public policy was said, by Lord Reid in *Rondel* v. *Worsley* [1969] 1 AC 191 at p. 227, to be the basis of the rule that a barrister was immune from an action of negligence by his client in respect of the conduct of litigation.

4 In *Regents of University of California* v. *Bakke*, 438 US 265 (1978) Powell J. seeking to 'interpret' and apply the words 'No person . . . shall . . . be subjected to *discrimination*'

said, 'The concept of "discrimination" is susceptible of varying interpretations, for as Mr Justice Holmes declared, '[a] word is not a crystal, transparent and unchanged, it is the skin of a living thought and may vary greatly in colour and content according to the circumstances and the time in which it is used'.

5 The framers of the constitution did not address their minds to 'wire-tapping'; but the Supreme Court has repeatedly had to decide what the constitution decides about wire-tapping. So in *Olmstead* v. *United States* 277 US 438 (1928) it was held (by 5 votes to 4) that evidence of private telephone conversations obtained by illegal wire-tapping could be admitted in a criminal trial notwithstanding the Fourth Amendment prohibition against unreasonable searches and the Fifth Amendment prohibition of compulsory self-incrimination. Olmstead and others were using the telephone in connection with running a huge business of importing and selling prohibited liquor. But the *Olmstead* case was gradually 'so eroded by our subsequent decisions that the "trespass" doctrine here enunciated can no longer be regarded as controlling': *Katz* v. *United States* 398 US 347 (1967). Likewise the framers of the Constitution knew nothing of 'primary' elections, used by political parties to choose who should be candidates in actual elections. But in many States where one party enjoyed permanent political dominance the primary elections were all that mattered because *de facto* whoever succeeded in the primary was bound to be elected. Although the Constitution, as amended, rendered unconstitutional any state law preventing blacks from voting in the actual election, it contained nothing about the rights of blacks to vote in primaries. The court had to rationalise into the Constitution a right that those who wrote it could not have had in contemplation (*Smith* v. *Allwright* 321 US 649).

6 *Marbury* v. *Madison*, 5 US 39 (1803). There is, of course, an enormous literature about whether the Constitution intended the judges to decide what the Constitution intended. The judges decided that the Constitution intended that the judges should decide what the Constitution intended. It will be seen that this is the constitutional equivalent of auto levitation. How it was done, how the naked emperor acquired a wardrobe, is best explained by Robert G. McCloskey in *The American Supreme Court* (The University of Chicago Press, 1960). Chief Justice Hughes said, 'the Constitution is what the judges say it is', quoted, Schwartz (American Constitutional Law) p. 130. Ultimately, of course, the judges get away with auto-levitation if the political power is prepared to tolerate it. Nobody knew what would happen next if President Nixon had chosen to disobey the Supreme Court over the Watergate tapes (*United States* v. *Nixon* 418 US 683 (1974)): no court can *enforce* its orders against the ultimate civil power. The case is discussed by Laurence H. Tribe, Tyler Professor of Constitutional Law at Harvard, in *God Save This Honorable Court* (Random House, New York) p. 5.

7 Daniel Boorstin, Librarian of Congress and sometime Reith Lecturer, in his preface to *The American Supreme Court*, by McCloskey, op. cit.

8 *Katz* v. *United States (supra)*.

9 *Buck* v. *Bell* 274 US 200 (1927) held that the mentally sub-normal could be sterilised without their consent: they were classified as mentally defective on the basis of IQ tests that would not be regarded as reliable today. Holmes, delivering the Opinion of the Court said: 'It is better for all the world if, instead of waiting to execute degenerate offspring for crime, or to let them starve for imbecility, society can prevent those who are manifestly unfit from continuing their kind.

10 *West Coast Hotel* v. *Parrish* 300 US 379 (1937).

11 *Loving* v. *Virginia* 388 US 1 (1967) in which the court held that Virginia's statutory scheme to prevent marriage between persons solely on the basis of racial classification violated the Equal Protection and Due Process Clauses of the Fourteenth Amendment. Fifteen other States had similar miscegenation statutes.

12 c.f. *Furman* v. *Georgia (supra); Woodson* v. *North Carolina* 428 US 280 (1976); *Gregg* v. *Georgia* 428 US 153 (1976).

13 *Griswold* v. *Connecticut* 381 US 479 (1965). The Supreme Court, on procedural grounds, put off until 1972 a decision as to whether or not single women had a constitutional right to obtain and use contraceptives. It was then decided that they had such a right: *Eisenstadt* v. *Baird* 405 US 438 (1972).

14 *United States* v. *Nixon* 418 US 683 (1974). This case in which the court unanimously rejected the President's claim to be above the law (the doctrine of 'executive privilege') is summarised, against its background, in *Storm Center* by David M. O' Brien (W. W. Norton & Company, Newport, London) at pp. 215–22. The layman may prefer the highly readable, though not authoritative, account in *The Brethren* by Woodward and Armstrong (op. cit.) pp. 289 *et seq.*

15 *Roe* v. *Wade* 410 US 113 (1973). For the background and some of the repercussions, see O'Brien *Storm Center* op. cit., Chapt. 1. The battle over abortion continues. As the court can overrule its previous decisions it may yet change the law, redefining what the elected legislatures may or may not do.

16 *Baker* v. *Carr* 399 US 186 (1962), and *Reynolds* v. *Sims* 377 US 533 (1964), which resulted in States and local governments having to provide equal voting rights to individuals.

17 *West Virginia State Board of Education* v. *Barnette* 319 US 624 (1943), reversing *Minersville School District* v. *Gobitis* 310 US 586 (1940); in the result, schoolchildren cannot be compelled to salute the flag and recite the pledge of allegiance because such compulsion breaches the First Amendment guarantee of freedom of religion.

18 *Plessy* v. *Ferguson* 163 US 537 (1896) (giving rise to the 'separate but equal' doctrine, thus allowing enforced segregation).

19 *Brown* v. *Board of Education (No. 1)* 347 US 483 (1954) which, to all intents and purposes, overruled *Plessy* v. *Ferguson*.

20 *Bradwell* v. *Illinois* 83 US 16 Wall 130 (1873), holding constitutional a State law preventing women from practising law in the State. Bradley J. declared that the 'paramount destiny and mission of women are to fulfill the whole and benign offices of wife and mother. This is the law of the Creator'. This is a favourite quotation of Justice Sandra Day O'Connor, whose elevation to the Court in 1981 by President Reagan gave the lie to another of Bradley's *dicta*. 'The natural and proper timidity and delicacy which belongs to the female sex evidently unfits it for many of the occupations of civil life.'

21 *Miranda* v. *Arizona* 384 US 436 (1966).

22 *Mapp* v. *Ohio* 367 US 643 (1961).

23 The prevailing Scottish rules were to be found in *Chalmers* v. *HM Advocate* 1954 SC

(J) 66 where a full Bench (of five judges) held that the trial judge should exclude evidence, for example of an alleged confession, if he considered that the legal safeguards had not been observed. That case and *HM Advocate* v. *Rigg* 1946 SC (J) 1 show that the Scottish Court, as then constituted, viewed with unease and distaste the frequency with which the prosecution produced what were said to be voluntary statements made spontaneously to policemen by persons in police custody. Although today the law remains the same the emphasis has changed; the test to be applied is one of 'fairness' and, unless there has been some flagrant breach of established safeguards, the jury is to be allowed to hear the evidence and to be told that the evidence may be taken into account if it was not unfairly obtained. *Hartley* v. *HM Advocate,* 1979 SLT 26; *Lord Advocate's Reference No. 1 of 1983,* 1984 SLT 337. The result is to diminish the role of the judge in excluding evidence that may be tainted by the use of improper methods. The position in England is different again: The law was carefully considered in *Reg.* v. *Sang* [1980] AC 402 where it was said *obiter* that although a trial judge always had a discretion to exclude evidence if his subjective sense of fairness and justice so required, he had no discretion to exclude relevant evidence merely because it had been obtained by improper or unfair means. Lord Diplock clearly distinguished between the English approach and the Scottish or American approach by saying, 'It is no part of a judge's function to exercise disciplinary powers over the police or prosecution as respects the way evidence to be used at the trial is obtained by them'. In *Chalmers*, Lord Cooper virtually said the opposite: 'We have no power to give instructions to the police, but we have the power and the duty to exclude from the cognisance of a jury evidence which, according to our practice and decisions is inadmissible; and the police have an interest to know why such decisions are taken.' In his magnificent and liberal opinion in *Miranda* Chief Justice Warren approved and endorsed the Scottish approach, quoting *Chalmers*; and disapproved the notion that the interest of society in convicting the guilty should prevail over procedures designed to safeguard civil rights – quoting Brandeis, 'To declare that in the administration of the criminal law the end justifies the means . . . would bring terrible retribution. Against that pernicious doctrine this Court should resolutely set its face'. The legislature has recently stepped into this field with ss 76–78 of the Police and Criminal Evidence Act, 1984, which contain complicated provisions applicable to England and Wales only about the admissibility of confessions and of evidence which might have 'an adverse effect on the fairness of the proceedings.' Nobody yet knows how these new statutory provisions will work. The trouble with the notion of 'fairness' to which the English and Scottish Courts now have to pay so much attention is that it is wholly vague and subjective. Lord Diplock, in *Reg* v. *Sang* (p. 431) said, 'What is unfair, what is trickery in the context of the detection and prevention of crime, are questions which are liable to attract highly subjective answers'. Lord Fraser of Tullybelton (p. 450) agreed that the use of words like 'unfair or oppressive' introduces 'standards which are largely subjective and which are therefore liable to variation. But I do not think there is any cause for anxiety in that . . . Judges are accustomed . . . to applying . . . standards containing a large subject element.' A different perspective, in the constitutional context, was adopted by Judge Learned Hand, who, in The Bill of Rights (Harvard University Press, Cambridge, Massachusetts, 1958) wrote (p. 70), '. . . judges . . . wrap up their veto in a protective veil of adjectives such as 'arbitrary,' 'artificial,' 'normal,' 'reasonable,' ''fundamental,' or 'essential,' whose office usually, though quite innocently, is to disguise what they are doing and impute to it a derivation far more impressive than their personal preferences, which are all that in fact lies behind the decision.'

24 This was what worried Justice White who dissented in *Miranda* saying, 'Much of the trouble with the court's new rule is that it will operate indiscriminately in all criminal cases, regardless of the severity of the crime or the circumstances involved. It applies to every defendent, whether the professional criminal or one committing a crime of momentary passion who is not part and parcel of organised crime. It will slow down the investigation and apprehension of confederates in those cases where time is of the essence such as . . . kidnapping . . . espionage . . . organised crime . . . For all these reasons . . . a more flexible approach makes much more sense than the Court's constitutional straitjacket which forecloses more discriminating treatment by legislative or rule-making pronouncements.'

25 The recent (March 4, 1985) case of *Oregon* v. *Elstad*, 105 S Ct. 1285 is an example of the narrowing down of the protection afforded by the *Miranda* decision. In *Elstad* the police obtained an incriminating statement from a suspect who had not been informed of his constitutional rights (as required by *Miranda*). Then, at the police station, he was given the *Miranda* warning and executed a written confession. The written confession was admitted in evidence though the earlier spoken statement was excluded. The majority (6:3) in the Supreme Court took the view that the second occasion could be separated from the first sufficiently to allow the suspect's decision to give a written confession to be regarded as a separate act of free will by a person properly informed of his rights. Contrast with *Chalmers* v. *HM Advocate* 1954 SC (J) 66 where a Full Bench (5 judges) held that two such separate occasions fell to be regarded as 'part and parcel of the same transaction' so that the taint which affected the first also affected the second.

26 An interesting inroad into what some would regard as an inviolable constitutional right, the right to silence, was made by the Criminal Justice (Scotland) Act, 1980, s 6 which allows an accused person to be questioned by the Procurator-Fiscal in front of the Sheriff. The questions relate to his alleged involvement in the crime in respect of which he has been arrested. He is not obliged to answer but his failure to do so may be the subject of explicit, adverse comment at his subsequent trial.

27 In a discussion of the AIDS problem in Harvard Law Review, Vol. 99, 1986 (p. 1274) these and other examples of measures introduced by legislatures and public health authorities are given. In the light of many court rulings about the degree to which public health measures (usually applying to the public generally or to a discrete class – such as 'Asians' or 'prostitutes' or 'tuberculosis patients') impair civil liberties, the author concludes that many such measures now being taken to limit the spread of Aids would be 'constitutionally inadequate'. In the Irish Republic where there are constitutional restrictions regarding contraception a campaign to encourage the use of condoms would presumably be unlawful.

28 In *Miliangos* v. *Frank (Textiles) Ltd* [1976] AC 443 the House of Lords reversed a rule that had stood for centuries, namely that any damages awarded by a Court to a foreign plaintiff had to be assessed in sterling according to the rate of exchange prevailing at the date when the payment was due, not at the date of the Court's judgment. The House of Lords, since 1966, had the right to reverse or not follow its own precedent; but the Court of Appeal had no right to fail to follow a binding Lord's precedent. Their doing so resulted in what Lord Wilberforce called 'some distortion of the judicial process' (p. 459).

29 Lord Scarman in *English Law: The New Dimension* writes that the system of judicial precedent was 'made flexible by judiciary artistry in "distinguishing" cases and judicial

skill in selecting not only the law applicable to the facts of a case, but sometimes the facts as well (e.g. the judicial phrase "the relevant facts").'

30 HL Deb, Vol. 457, col. 1120/1 (1977).

31 Learned Hand's words are quoted by Archibald Cox (p. 21) in *Storm Over the Supreme Court*, Blumenthal Memorial Lecture, February 13, 1986, in which he develops the argument that even although one might approve of the results of unfettered judicial activism it is more important that the judges themselves are subject to the law. A liberal court can be succeeded by a reactionary court; it is then too late for liberals to start complaining about the absence of restraint by judges.

5 AN ENORMOUS POWER

1 Canada Act 1982 enacting and bringing into force for Canada the Constitution Act, 1982.

2 Section 15(1) of the Constitution Act, 1982, provides, 'Every individual is equal before and under the law and has the right to the equal protection and equal benefit of the law without discrimination and, in particular, without discrimination based on race, national or ethnic origin, colour, religion, sex, age or mental or physical disability'. Subsection (2) specifically permits any positive discrimination law program or activity designed to ameliorate the conditions of the disadvantaged. This provision should help to avoid the kind of problem seen in the United States, for example in *Regents of the University of California* v. *Bakke*, 438 US 265 (1978), holding that quota systems specifically to assist the disadvantaged (racially disadvantaged) to enter college were unconstitutional. See also *United Steel Workers of America* v. *Weber*, (1979), 49 S. Ct. 2721.

3 Senator Eugene Forsey is quoted (in 'Canada's Charter of Rights and Freedoms' in 'Public Law', an Article by Randolph Hahn, at p. 531) as predicting that the Charter would be, 'a field day for crackpots, a pain in the neck for judges and legislators, and a goldmine for lawyers'. The comments are quoted from a Public Address at the University of Calgary in October 1983 and are cited by F. L. Morton in 'Changing the Charter – Year 1: a statistical analysis' a Paper given at the 1984 Annual Meeting of the Canadian Political Science Association, University of Guelph, June 10, 1984.

4 In the third Richard O'Sullivan lecture, delivered on May 26, 1977, Lord Hailsham of St Marylebone said '. . . it has come to be realised that Parliament itself can be made an instrument of tyranny.' In Answer 39 in evidence before the Select Committee of the House of Lords on a Bill of Rights (June 20, 1977) he said, 'If you are to deal with what I regard as elected dictatorship, you would have to go very much outside the terms of reference of this Bill.' The Bill referred to was Lord Wade's Bill, then before the House of Lords, to introduce the European Convention on Human Rights into British Law. In *The Lawful Rights of Mankind* (Oxford University Press, 1985), Paul Sieghart attributes the notion of the 'tyranny of the majority' to Alexis de Tocqueville (p. 41).

5 In a lecture to the Minority Rights Group delivered in November 1977 (and reprinted in the Minutes of Evidence taken before the House of Lords' Select Committee on a Bill of Rights) Lord Scarman described a Bill of Rights as 'imperative'. In a Note for the Committee he said 'The UK requires a new constitutional settlement, and . . . a Bill of Rights should be included in the settlement.' This continues his advocacy of such a course contained in the Hamlyn lectures, 1974, *English Law: The New Dimension* (Stevens).

6 The same conclusion was reached by the specialist adviser (D. Rippengal) to the House of Lords' Select Committee, HMSO 1977 (81) p. 1. Lord Diplock agreed with him (Question 164).

7 The clearest finding to that effect is contained in the *Dred Scott* case, *Scott* v. *Sandford*, 60 US 393 (1857), which some believe hastened the movement towards the Civil War: cf. *Storm Center op. cit.* David M. O'Brien. The history of discrimination in Canada against various ethnic minorities including native peoples, Acadians, Metis, Japanese and Chinese immigrants, and various religious minorities, including especially Jehovah's Witnesses, is surveyed and summarised by Ed. Ratushny in *Security in the Multi-Ethnic State: The Canadian Experience* (a paper prepared for a conference in Colombo, Sri Lanka in February 1984, sponsored by The Marga Institute). He says (p. 13), 'Generally, where a threat to the security of the state has been perceived, whether political, religious or racial in origin, governments have responded with oppressive measures and with little regard for the attendant abrogation of civil liberties'. He makes it clear that this is equally true of the United States.

8 In *Somerset* v. *Stewart* (1772) Lofft. 1.21 How. St. Tr. 1 it was decided that slavery was illegal in England (and it was noted to be illegal in Scotland). That decision did not apply to the English Colonies, including North America, where slavery continued to flourish.

9 'A Bill of Rights for New Zealand'. A White Paper, presented to the House of Representatives by leave of the Hon. Geoffrey Palmer, Minister of Justice, para. 4.24.

10 'Trends and Prospects in The United States Supreme Court', Article in *Public Law*, Spring 1986, by Norman Dorsen, Stokes Professor of Law, New York University Law School, p. 89.

11 Canadian Charter of Rights and Freedoms, Sec. 1 (Schedule B to the Canada Act, 1982).

12 The average age of the judges of High Court rank and above is in the mid-sixties (cf. report in the 'Independent', January 12, 1987). When applying the common law all judges look back at precedent to see how the problem, or a similar problem, was approached and solved in the past, sometimes in the very distant past. In the common law countries they usually apply the policy or doctrine of *stare decisis*, the policy of deciding the instant case in the same way as the precedent, without thinking out the problem afresh, on the principle, articulated by Brandeis, '. . . in most matters it is more important that the applicable rule of law be *settled* than it be settled *right*'. *Burnet* v. *Coronado Oil* 285 US 393 (1932) pp. 406–8; cf. also Lord Halsbury's speech in *London Street Tramways Co.* v. *LCC* [1898] AC 375. The House of Lords has announced that it will not regard itself as bound by its own precedents: See the Note (July 26, 1966) printed in [1966] 3 All ER p. 77. The previous position, stated by Lord Reid in *Chancery Lane Safe Deposit and Offices Co. Ltd* v. *Inland Revenue Comrs* [1966] AC 85, at p. 111, was 'This House still regards itself as bound by the rule that it must not reverse or depart from a previous decision of the House.'

13 In the Irish fluoridation case, *Ryan* v. *A-G* 1965 IR 294, Kenny, J. found support for the existence, beyond the constitution, of a 'right to bodily integrity' in the Encyclical Letter of Pope John XXIII, 'Peace on Earth', April 11, 1963. A judge who is sufficiently learned or who is prepared to do enough research should be able to find supportive dicta somewhere for almost any proposition he considers it right to advance.

14 *Attorney-General* v. *Times Newspapers Ltd* [1974] AC 273.

15 The European Court of Human Rights made their decision by a majority of 11 votes to 9: *Sunday Times* v. *UK* [1979] 2 EHRR 245.

16 The Eighteenth Amendment prohibited the manufacture, sale, or transportation, importation or exportation of intoxicating liquors.

17 The Twenty-first Amendment repealed the Eighteenth Amendment.

18 The New Zealand White Paper says (S 3.14) '. . . the Bill would leave to the unfolding operation of (our) constitutional and political system the selection and resolution of the debates in society about substantive values, especially in the economic area. Accordingly, the Bill does not include major economic, social and cultural rights'.

19 The concept of selecting rights and duties from behind a 'veil of ignorance', being ignorance as to how the selection would benefit or disbenefit the interests of the selectors, is developed by John Rawls in *A Theory of Justice* (Cambridge, Belknap Press of Harvard University Press, 1971) Chapter III, para. 24, pp. 136 *et seq.* In *The Lawful Rights of Mankind* (Oxford University Press, 1985) Paul Sieghart develops in Chap. 1, 'An Allegory' the notion of rational beings evolving a system of legal rights which balance competing interests, as they emerge, by rational civilised discussion.

20 In *Roe* v. *Wade* 410 US 113 (1973) the US Supreme Court, by a majority, held that Texas Criminal Statutes, making it a crime to procure an abortion, except for the purpose of saving the mother's life, were unconstitutional because they violated a woman's right to privacy in the Due Process Clause of the Fourteenth Amendment (Adopted in 1868). The relevant parts of the Fourteenth Amendment provide: 'No State shall make . . . any law which shall abridge the privileges or immunities of citizens of the United States; nor shall any State deprive any person of life, liberty or property, without due process of law . . .' It will be observed that these words say nothing expressly about abortion. More strikingly, they say nothing at all about a right to privacy. The court, however, found that 'the penumbras' of the Bill of Rights included a right to privacy which had been recognised by the court in assorted cases since 1891 and that that right of privacy 'is broad enough to encompass a woman's decision whether or not to terminate her pregnancy' (p. 153). A 'fetus', the court concluded, was not a 'person' within the meaning of the Fourteenth Amendment. If a fetus was a 'person' the court observed, the Texas statute, like others which allow abortion to save the mother's life, would itself run foul of the due process clause. In this context, the outsider can see the force of the observation of Rehnquist, J. (dissenting, and now Chief Justice), 'To reach its result, the court necessarily has had to find within the scope of the Fourteenth Amendment a right that was apparently unknown to the drafters of the Amendment.' The Texas statute was first enacted eleven years before the Fourteenth Amendment was adopted. It is hardly suprising that *Roe* v. *Wade* is not regarded by the opponents of abortion as the last word on the matter. The history of the continuing battle can be studied in *Storm Center op. cit.* pp. 23–43. A layman's account of the background to the making of the decision can be found in *The Brethren op. cit.* 165–89 and pp. 229–40.

21 The European Court of Human Rights considered the effect of Article 11 of the European Convention in *Young, James and Webster* v. *UK* [1982] 4 EHRR 38. Article 11 says that everyone has the right to 'freedom of association with others including the right to form and join trade unions for the protection of his interests'. The court did not go as

far as to hold that this provision necessarily made the closed shop illegal in all cases; but, in the case under consideration, the threat of dismissal directed against the three British Rail employees, who had entered that employment before British Rail concluded the closed shop agreement with the three rail unions, was held to be a most serious form of compulsion striking at the very substance of the freedom guaranteed by Article 11. Undue pressure on workmen to join a particular trade union was held to interfere with the associated right to protection of personal opinion afforded by other Articles of the European Convention, (Articles 9 and 10). The court went on to hold that the restriction of the Article 11 freedom of association could not be justified as 'necessary in a free society.'

22 *First National Bank of Boston* v. *Belloti* 435 US 765 (1978). The court had regarded corporations as 'persons' within the meaning of the Fourteenth Amendment since the late 19th Century: *Santa Clara County* v. *Southern Pacific Rly. Co.* 118 US 394 (1886): the court did not even allow argument about this question, and, without argument, decided it unanimously. Accordingly, a corporation is entitled to freedom of speech as guaranteed by the First Amendment. Hence a Massachusetts Criminal Statute, prohibiting banks and business corporations from spending money to influence the voters in a forthcoming referendum about the introduction of a graduated personal income tax, was held to be unconstitutional.

23 In *Campbell and Cosans* v. *United Kingdom* [1982] 4 EHRR 293, the European Court of Human Rights held that state schools which suspended pupils whose parents objected to the schools' practice and policy of using corporal punishment, if necessary, to discipline pupils were violating the rights of parents under Article 2 of Protocol No. 1 of the European Convention. That Article reads, 'No person shall be denied the right to education. In the exercise of any functions which it assumes in relation to education and to teaching, the State shall respect the right of parents to ensure such education and teaching in conformity with their own religious and philosophical convictions.' Whether anyone envisaged, when drafting or agreeing to these words, that they would necessitate the provision of separate educational facilities for children whose parents objected to corporal punishment is exceedingly doubtful. The dissenting Judge (Sir Vincent Evans) argues convincingly that the court's interpretation is too wide (i.e. the authors did not mean what the judges held them to mean).

24 In *Nebraska Press Association* v. *Stuart* 427 US 539 (1976) the freedom of the press was allowed to prevail over the right of an accused person to have a trial unaffected by pre-trial publicity.

25 *The Americans: A New History of the People of the United States* (Little, Brown and Company, Boston-Toronto) by Oscar Handlin, p. 336.

26 Possibly the clearest issues to illustrate the difference between a Bill of Rights country and one where Parliament is sovereign are abortion and the death penalty. In the United States they are constitutional issues decided by judges, their decisions liable to be overturned by other judges. In the United Kingdom they are political issues, decided by elected members of the House of Commons and able to be reviewed, in the light of changing circumstances, perceptions and pressures, by the same or different members of the House of Commons. The Reagan Administration which is opposed to the ruling given in *Roe* v. *Wade* (recognising the constitutional right of a woman to choose to have an abortion) has to seek to argue in other cases before the court that *Roe* v. *Wade* should

be reversed. Senator Orrin G. Hatch, in the Harvard Law Review, Vol. 99, at p. 1349 quotes from the brief lodged by the United States in *Thornburgh* v. *American College of Obstetricians and Gynecologists,* 105 S. Ct. 2015 (1985) urging the Court to 'reconsider' and 'abandon' *Roe* v. *Wade*. There is little doubt that in nominating Justices to the Supreme Court the administration attaches particular importance to the candidates' views on the abortion and death penalty issues. The present Chief Justice (Rehnquist) is quoted by Professor Tribe (*God Save This Honorable Court*, page X) as saying in October 1984 that he saw 'no reason in the world why a President should not' try to select judges to reflect the President's perspective in their decision-making. The U.S. Attorney-General, Edwin Meese, is the most articulate protagonist of the view that the Supreme Court should adopt the Reagan 'social agenda', and that only judges with what he calls 'the proper judicial philosophy and approach' should be appointed to the federal bench: c.f. article in ABA Journal, February 1, 1987, 'The Policy and Rhetoric of Ed. Meese.'

27 The Scottish Courts eventually produced a satisfactory solution in *Hall* v. *Associated Newspapers Ltd.* 1979 SC (J) 1 in which it was held that the court's jurisdiction with regard to contempt of court runs from the moment of arrest or, if earlier, from the moment the court grants a warrant to arrest. From that point of time the accused person is under the care and protection of the court and therafter the publication of any material which may be regarded as prejudicial to a fair and impartial trial may be treated as contempt of court. This ruling was in effect enacted for the United Kingdom by The Contempt of Court Act, 1981.

28 In *Law and Lawyers in the United States* (Stevens, 1964) Elwin N. Griswold, Dean and Langdell Professor of Law, Harvard Law School, wrote (p. 117): '"Separate but equal" on trains and buses, and in schools, meant, in practice, racial discrimination of the clearest sort . . . This was the period when I was a boy, when I was studying the history of the United States – the Declaration of Independence, with its affirmation that 'all men are created equal,' the Civil War, with the freeing of the slaves, and the adoption of the great provisions of the Thirteenth, Fourteenth and Fifteenth Amendments. . . . But I could see signs of discrimination all around me; and I learned about such things as the Civil Rights Cases, and *Plessy* v. *Ferguson*, and I was puzzled. Ours is a great country, with great traditions. We have claimed to be the home of liberty, and we went through a Revolution from the Mother Country to provide that liberty, and through the fire of a Civil War to preserve and extend that liberty. And what had we done with it? These were puzzling questions to me as a student. They did not become any clearer to me as a young lawyer.'

29 In the *Miranda* case (*Miranda* v. *Arizona* 384 US 436 (1966) Chief Justice Warren reviewed cases and other sources illustrating how police violence and 'third degree' methods against suspects detained for interrogation 'flourished' in the United States and how the resort to physical brutality was continuing. He cites examples of beating, hanging, whipping suspects to obtain confessions and refers to a recent case in which the police 'brutally beat, kicked and placed lighted cigarette butts on the back of a potential witness under interrogation for the purpose of securing a statement incriminating a third party', adding, 'The examples given above are undoubtedly the exception now, but they are sufficiently widespread to be the object of concern.' Some confessions so obtained were still being admitted as evidence in criminal trials.

30 Marshall, J. in *Regents of the University of California* v. *Bakke,* 438 US 265 (1975), at p. 387. In 'Trends and Prospects in the United States Supreme Court' Public Law,

Spring 1986, Norman Dorsen writes, (page 84) 'The Supreme Court was not always a "palladium of justice" as Justice Hugo Black once called it. (*Illinois* v. *Allan,* 397 US 337, 346 (1970)). In the nineteenth century it was in fact a bastion of racism.'

31 *Lochner* v. *New York* 198 US 45 (1905) held that legislation to place a maximum limit on the number of hours that bakers could be required to work was a violation of 'due process' and unconstitutionally interfered with freedom of contract. The history of the application of *laissez-faire* principles is narrated in *The American Supreme Court* (op. cit.) by Robert G. McCloskey at pp. 153 *et seq.*

32 The *Dred Scott* case, *supra.*

33 *Plessy* v. *Ferguson, supra.*

34 E.g. in *Bradwell* v. *Illinois, supra.* Even the Warren Court held that a Florida statute which discriminated against women in relation to jury service was not unconstitutional: *Hoyt* v. *Florida* 368 US 57 (1961): '. . . woman is still regarded as the center of home and family life. We cannot say that it is constitutionally impermissible for a State, acting in pursuit of the general welfare, to conclude that a woman should be relieved from the civic duty of jury service unless she herself determines that such service is consistent with her own special responsibilities.' In the result, a woman accused of murdering her husband, could be tried by an all-male jury.

35 *Korematsu* v. *US* 323 US 214 (1944) holding that curfews, detention camps and assorted restrictions on movement were permitted by the constitution even although, as Jackson, J. pointed out the only fact that made *Korematsu* guilty of anything was the fact of his Japanese ancestry. In ABA Journal, Vol. 72, July 1, 1986, it is reported (p. 24) that Korematsu's conviction for a curfew violation was vacated in 1984 by a federal district court in San Francisco, and the Justice Department did not appeal. The assertions upon which the government based its regulations and defended them proved to be without substance. Even libertarian judges joined in the restriction of constitutional rights under wartime pressures. One example is Douglas J. Chief Justice Burger, paying tribute to him shortly after his death said,

> 'Douglas' votes in the Japanese cases, which also appear somewhat anomalous in view of his subsequent history, may have a different or additional basis. In 1943, he voted with the majority in condoning the indiscriminate interment of Japanese; a year later he joined Justice Black's majority opinion sanctioning exclusion of a Japanese from his home town in California. In his separate opinion in the 1943 case *Hirabayashi* v. *United States,* 320 US 81, 106 (1943), he explained his vote: It was wartime; Pearl Harbour had been bombed; and Douglas was unwilling to "sit in judgment on the military requirements of that hour. . . ." He later characterized the decisions in the two cases as "extreme."' 449 US p. XV, November 18, 1980.

Canada took similar measures; *Co-operative Committee on Japanese Canadians* v. *Attorney-General for Canada,* [1947] AC 87. So did the United Kingdom: Defence (General) Regulations, 1939, reg. 18B, *cf. Liversidge* v. *Anderson* [1943] AC 206; but in Canada and the United Kingdom the restrictions were authorised by Parliament. In Canada the restrictions endured until 1949, by which time thousands of Japanese Canadians – many born in Canada, had been deported to Japan. Not one was ever even charged with espionage. It is not my purpose to suggest that such restrictive measures were unwarranted in the circumstances of wartime; I merely point out that even the supreme law of an entrenched Bill of Rights yields under pressure.

36 The European Court of Luxembourg does for some purposes at least enforce within the EEC the principles of the European Convention in applying community law: see Opinion of Lord Ross in *Kaur* v. *Lord Advocate* 1980 SC 319. In the judgment in *Internationale Handelsgesellschaft mbH* v. *Einfuhr & Vorratsstelle für Getreide & Futtermittel* [1972] CMLR 255 the Court said, 'For respect for fundamental rights has an integral part in the general principles of law of which the Court of Justice ensures respect. The protection of such rights, while inspired by the constitutional principles common to the Member-States must be ensured within the framework of the Community's structure and objectives' (p. 283).

6 LIONS UNDER THE THRONE

1 Oliver Wendell Holmes, *The Common Law* (1881) (Macmillan, 1968) p. 1: 'The life of the law has not been logic: it has been experience. The felt necessities of the time, the prevalent moral and political theories, intuitions of public policy, avowed or unconscious, even the prejudices which judges share with their fellow-men, have had a good deal more to do than the syllogism in determining the rules by which men should be governed.'

2 In *Storm Center* (op. cit.) (p. 236), David O'Brien gives this example from the Supreme Court: 'Personal animosities sometimes prevail. The most extreme were those of Justice McReynolds. He was anti-Semitic, and whenever Brandeis spoke at conference, he would get up from his chair and go out of the conference room. But he would leave the door open a crack and peek in till Brandeis was through, and then he would come back and take his seat.' McReynolds served on the court for 27 years, and Brandeis for 23 of the same years. Another form of prejudice is a Cromwellian confidence in one's own political and social perspective; after he died at the age of 98, it was said of Lord Halsbury, a Lord Chancellor active both politically and judicially, sometimes both at the same time, 'He had been a great political figure, and never wavered when he thought he was in the right. His greatest fault, perhaps, was that he never thought he was in the wrong.' (R. Stevens, *Law and Politics: The House of Lords as a Judicial Body*, 1800-1976 (1979) p. 120, Note 71, quoted Edward Russell, *The Royal Conscience*). Many judges get a reputation for being biased in favour of the prosecution in criminal cases or for being a plaintiffs' judge or a defendants' in reparation cases. But this is difficult to demonstrate statistically. In the USA academics do study the judges' decisions to try to discover preference or bias. But in the UK 'jurimetrics', as such study is called, would not get much encouragement from the Bench.

3 Laurence Tribe illustrates how common 5–4 decisions are in *God Save the Honorable Court* p. 32 and records, 'About one-fifth of the court's cases in the decade from 1974 to 1984 were decided on a 5–4 basis.'

4 *Miranda* v. *Arizona*, 384 US 436 (1966).

5 367 US 643 (1961).

6 This is obviously an over-simple precis of Powell, J's position which occupies 55 pages in a report which extends to 156 pages. In discussing the *Bakke* case, O'Brien, *Storm Center* op. cit. at p. 26, refers to one group of four justices as 'the Stevens bloc'; the opposing group of four was 'the Brennan bloc'. For one part of his Opinion, Powell voted with the Stevens bloc 'that quota systems were invalid and that Bakke should be admitted'. For the other part – that certain types of 'affirmative-action programs' were

constitutionally permissible – he agreed with the Brennan bloc. In the end, therefore, as O'Brien says, 'Powell's pragmatic rationalization for the controversial decision thus had the support of no other justice'. *Regents of the University of California* v. *Bakke*, 438 US 265 (1978). The most recent cases on affirmative action are discussed by Neal Devins in the ABA Journal, February 1, 1987, p. 44 *et seq*.

7 *Brown* v. *Board of Education (1st case)* 347 US 483 (1954).

8 The full story of this most famous 'might have been' is repeated in numerous works; cf. *The Unpublished Opinions of the Warren Court* (Oxford University Press) Bernard Schwartz, (p. 445) in which the author narrates how Chief Justice Vinson would have voted to uphold the 'separate but equal' doctrine (cf. *Plessy* v. *Ferguson*). When he learned that Vinson had suddenly died, Frankfurter, J. said, 'This is the first indication I have ever had that there is a God.'

9 The history of President Roosevelt's encounters with the Supreme Court is summarised in Chap. 2 of *The President and the Supreme Court* by John D. Lees, BAAS pamphlets in American studies, 3. Lees also illustrates how the control of appointments to the Supreme Court became one of the most important political issues in America. See also Chap. VI, 'The Judiciary and the Welfare State' in *The American Supreme Court* (op. cit.) by Robert G. McCloskey.
The Brethren (op. cit.) p. 10. As President, Nixon announced, and pursued, a policy of appointing to the Supreme Court only strict constructionists, i.e. judges whose basic canon of interpretation would be to take out of the Constitution no more than its authors could be shown to have intended to put it.

10 Once the 1980 election was over the President of the American Bar Association wrote about 'the unfortunate tendency of American politicians to involve the judiciary in their campaigns; the quotation he gives is taken from the Republican Party's 'platform'.

11 Also 66 ABA Journal President's Page (p. 1318) (1980).

12 President Reagan has appointed two Justices, Sandra Day O'Connor (1981) and Antonin Scalia (1986) and promoted Rehnquist, J. to be Chief Justice. President (Franklin) Roosevelt appointed eight, and promoted Stone, J. to be Chief Justice: as a result, for almost a decade at least seven of his nominees sat together. President Nixon appointed four, including Chief Justice Burger. On the other hand, President Carter appointed none.

13 Professor O'Brien (*Storm Center*, p. 67) says, 'The Presidential impulse to pack the Court with politically compatible justices is irresistible.' After the first, Hugo Black (1937), his later appointments 'all turned on the ideological litmus test of support for the New Deal.' (O'Brien. 70). Laurence Tribe's book, *God Save This Honorable Court* is a plea directed at the Senate to exercise its powers to withhold consent if necessary to prevent the court from becoming unbalanced. The Senate, though it questions nominees, seldom votes decisively to reject them. Only four nominees have been refused Senate confirmation since 1894: Orrin G. Hatch in 'Save The Court From What?' in Harvard Law Review, Vol. 99, p. 1347, dismissing Tribe's book as politically prejudiced. It would be difficult to refute that assessment because Presidents are so powerfully influenced by political considerations in selecting judges for the highest feudal courts that any attempts to curb the Presidents' power is inevitably political in character.

14 In *Law and Politics, The House of Lords as a Judicial Body, 1800–1976* (Weidenfield and

Nicolson, 1979), Robert Stevens illustrates (p. 85) the political selection of judges by two quotations from R. F. V. Henston's *Lives of the Lord Chancellors 1885–1940,* the first, from a letter by 'Lord Salisbury to Lord Halsbury, '[i]t is . . . the unwritten law of our party system; and there is no clearer statute in that unwritten law than the rule that party claims should always weigh very heavily in the disposal of the highest legal appointments. In dealing with them you cannot ignore the party system as you do in the choice of a general or an archbishop. It would be a breach of the tacit convention on which politicians and lawyers have worked the British Constitution together for the last 200 years'. The second, written by the Liberal Attorney-General (Sir William Robson) to the Prime Minister (Asquith) in 1910 included, 'The Lord Chancellor is no doubt anxious to exlude from his Court any appointment he believes to be political, but the political complexion of the Court cannot be altogether ignored especially in view of future developments. The tribunal would have to play a great part in disputes that are legal in form but political in fact, and it would be idle to deny the resolute bias of many of the judges – there and elsewhere. That bias will probably operate more than ever in cases that touch on labour, educational, constitutional and, for the future I might perhaps add, revenue questions.' Of the latter passage, Lord Roskill has recently said, 'Perhaps it would be too unkind to paraphrase this correspondence by saying that Robson meant 'there are too many Tories in the Lords: I am a Liberal; please appoint me.' Lord Roskill adds that for the next twenty years or so (till c. 1930) the recruitment of Law Lords was 'too often still based upon supposed political, rather than actual legal merit' – cf. his address to the Bentham Club, February 29, 1984, printed in *Current Legal Problems 1984*. The role of politics in the appointment of judges is comprehensively illustrated in *Judges on Trial* by Shimon Shetreet, (North Holland Publishing Company, 1976), especially at pp. 67 et. seq. The well-known political intrigue which brought the Attorney-General, Gordon Hewart, to office as Lord Chief Justice is described by Anthony Mockler in *Lions Under The Throne*, Chap. 18 'The Hewart Intrigue'. The author says that he took this version from the biography of Hewart: *The Chief* by Robert Jackson (Harrap, 1959). The idea was that an elderly judge would be appointed to keep the seat warm until the Prime Minister was ready to put his nominee in place. The scheme was of very doubtful legality and, of course, was kept secret. But it worked; in March 1922, when a general election seemed imminent the stop-gap Lord Chief Justice (Lawrence) resigned – it is said he did not know of his own resignation till he read it in *The Times* & Lloyd George then appointed Hewart.

15 It is inevitable that judges, reluctantly or not, decide such questions if they are raised in litigation. A good example is the issue of surrogate motherhood which judges have to decide on the basis of existing law while politicians discuss but do not get round to enacting legislation. Thus, in discussing a current American litigation about whether the surrogate mother or the biological father should have the right to bring up the child, *The Independent* (January 16, 1987) notes that so far twelve American States and the District of Columbia have debated the issues, without yet enacting any laws. The only legislation in the UK specifically addressed to this problem is the *Surrogacy Arrangements Act 1985*, which criminalises commercial surrogacy: see the Report of the Committee of Inquiry into Human Fertilisation and Embryology (1984) Cmnd 9314.

16 The method of appointing judges in England is discussed in *Judicial Appointments – the Lord Chancellor's Policies and Procedures*, HMSO, 1986. See also 'Refurbishing the Judicial Service' by Carol Harlow (Chap. 10 of *Public Law and Politics* (Ed. C. Harlow, Sweet &

Maxwell, 1986). In Scotland, the system is even more secretive. The Lord Advocate (a political minister) effectively chooses the new Senator. He consults with the Lord President of the Court of Session but is free to make up his own mind. When he recommends himself for appointment other more subtle factors come into play, but these are wrapped in mystery. Of the Scottish system, Shetreet (op. cit, p. 73), concludes 'It should be noted that although politics play a role in judicial appointment, the system has brought to the Bench outstanding lawyers.' That is true because many outstanding lawyers sought and obtained the office of Lord Advocate, one of the Great Offices of State. Outstanding lawyers would tend to arrive on the Bench, whatever routes were open to them.

17 Lord Keith of Kinkel, who was appointed a Senator of the College of Justice in 1971 by a Conservative administration, was appointed a Lord of Appeal in Ordinary by a Labour Administration in 1977.

18 The British judge on the European Court of Justice, Lord Mackenzie Stuart was appointed to that position in 1972, five months after his elevation to the Bench in Scotland; and both the British Advocate-Generals, Sir Jean-Pierre Warner (1972 and Sir Gordon Flynn (1981)) were appointed by Conservative Prime Ministers.

19 It has been said that the 'chief function of our judicial machinery is to ascertain the truth' *Estes* v. *Texas* 381 US 532 (1965). But that is true only if it is heavily qualified by acknowledging that many of our rules of procedure and evidence – such as the rule that a wife cannot usually be compelled to give evidence against her husband in a criminal trial, or the right of an accused person to remain silent, or the protection of 'confidential' relationships (e.g. solicitor and client) – act so as to put other interests above the ascertainment of the truth. The true view of the judge's role was stated by Lord Justice-Clerk Thomson in *Thomson* v. *Corporation of Glasgow,* 1962 SC (HL) 36 at p. 52. He said: 'Judges sometimes flatter themselves by thinking that their function is the ascertainment of truth. This is so only in a very limited sense. Our system of administering justice in civil affairs proceeds on the footing that each side, working at arm's length, selects its own evidence. Each side's selection of its own evidence may, for various reasons, be partial in every sense of the term. . . . It is on the basis of two carefully selected versions that the Judge is finally called upon to adjudicate. He cannot make investigations on his own behalf; he cannot call witnesses; his undoubted right to question witnesses who are put in the box has to be exercised with caution. He is at the mercy of contending sides whose whole object is not to discover truth but to get his judgment. That judgment must be based only on what he is allowed to hear. He may suspect that witnesses who know the 'truth' have never left the witness-room for the witness box because neither side dares risk them, but the most that he can do is to comment on their absence. . . . All litigation is in essence a trial of skill between opposing parties conducted under recognised rules, and the prize is the judge's decision. We have rejected inquisitorial methods and prefer to regard our judges as entirely independent. Like referees at boxing contests, they see that the rules are kept and count the points.'

20 S 101 of the Criminal Procedure (Scotland) Act, 1975, as substituted by the Criminal Justice (Scotland) Act, 1980, includes,

'(2) Subject to subsections . . . (4) and (5) below, an accused who is committed for any offence until liberated in due course of law shall not be detained by virtue of that committal for a total period of more than –

(b) 110 days, unless the trial of the case is commenced within that period, which failing he shall be liberated forthwith and thereafter he shall be for ever free of question or process for that offence.
(4) A single judge of the High Court may, on application made to him for the purpose, extend the period in subsection (2)(b) above where he is satisfied that delay in the commencement of the trial is due to –
(*a*) the illness of the accused or of a judge:
(*b*) the absence or illness of any necessary witness: or
(*c*) any other sufficient cause which is not attributable to any fault on the part of the prosecutor.
(5) The grant or refusal of any application to extend the periods mentioned in this section may be appealed against by note of appeal presented to the High Court; and that Court may affirm, reverse or amend the determination made on such application.
(6) For the purposes of this section, a trial shall be taken to commence when the oath is administered to the jury.'

21 From 1701 until 1981, the 110 days ran to the end of the trial so the trial had to be completed within 110 days of full committal. The 1980 Act, as will be seen from the previous note, required the trial to start by the 110th day. Under the old rule there were occasional acquittals if the prosecution failed to notice that time was running out. More commonly, the accused had to be released from custody to stop the 110 days from running: *HM Advocate* v. *McCann* 1977 JC1.

22 In *Law and Order*, the 1985 Hamlyn Lectures by Ralf Dahrendorf, (Stevens, 1985), the author, at p. 16, quotes Radzinowicz as guessing 'that only 15% of all crimes ever become fully known' and says that has 'since been largely confirmed by surveys of victims' (The Growth of Crime, Penguin Books) p. 63. In and after p. 17 he talks about the dark area of crime represented by *crimes* which are never discovered, and another dark area of discovered crimes the *perpetrators* of which are never detected. Obviously there is a certain amount of crime which is known about but is not reported and accordingly not detected. Thus for example victims of indecent assault are 'often unlikely to report the crime' (page 18). That is obviously equally true of much of the fraud and fiddling that goes on in business, shops, and the City.

23 Successive Lord Advocates announced that they would not prosecute consenting male adults in respect of private homosexual intercourse, despite the fact that this was a crime. See, for example, written answer by Solicitor General for Scotland to PQ No. 40 House of Commons Hansard, 9/7/80, Volume 988 at p. 211; see also HL Deb, Vol. 453, col. 1814 *et seq*. In *Keeping offenders out of Court: further alternatives to prosecution* (Cmnd 8958) Lord Stewart's Committee gives examples of criminal justice administration in the Netherlands and Scandinavia in which the public prosecutor may waive a prosecution. The Committee thought that the public prosecutor in Scotland should waive prosecutions more often than was in fact being done. Some prosecutions were waived in the 1970's in Scotland when Court Officials went on strike and the Courts could not have coped efficiently with the build up of untried cases.

23A This caustic comment on F. E. Smith (Lord Birkenhead) is attributed to Margot Asquith by John Campbell in 'F. E. Smith – First Earl of Birkenhead', (Jonathan Cape 1983), p. 616.

24 *The Lawful Rights of Mankind* Paul Sieghart, (Oxford University Press, 1985) at p. 29.

25 'Let judges also remember, that Solomon's throne was supported by lions on both sides. Let them be lions, but yet lions under the throne: being circumspect they do not check or oppose any points of sovereignty.' Francis Bacon,' Of Judicature, Essays Civil and Moral' – quoted in *Lions Under the Throne*, Anthony Mockler (Frederick Muller Ltd., 1983).

26 *Spirit of Liberty: Papers and Addresses of Learned Hand* (1953), (Dilliard ed., 1953).

TABLE OF CASES

•

TABLE OF STATUTES

INDEX